To the Shore of a Child's Ocean

Library and Archives Canada Cataloguing in Publication

Manning, Chris, 1965-
To the shore of a child's ocean / Chris Manning.

Includes bibliographical references.
Incomplete contents: pt. 1. Homeschooling from birth to age nine.
ISBN 978-0-9812236-0-5 (v. 1)

1. Home schooling. 2. Education—Parent participation.
I. Title.

LC40.M36 2009 371.04'2 C2009-904540-0

Artisan Pacific Publishing
Victoria, British Columbia
ArtisanPacificPublishing@gmail.com

Printed in USA

ISBN: 0-9812236-0-5
ISBN-13: 9780981223605

To order additional copies, please contact us.
BookSurge
www.booksurge.com
1-866-308-6235
orders@booksurge.com

To the Shore of a Child's Ocean

Part One:

Homeschooling from Birth to Age Nine

Chris Manning

APP
Artisan Pacific Publishing
Victoria, British Columbia
ArtisanPacificPublishing@gmail.com

Dedication

To our children who are about to set sail.

TABLE OF CONTENTS

ALSO BY CHRIS MANNING

George and Condi: The Last Decayed. *A Collection of Poems from the Last Decade*

Beaver Tales and a Canada Goosing: *Poems Illustrating a Uniquely Canadian Perspective*

ACKNOWLEDGEMENTS

What I have tried to do with this book is provide an honest, lucid account of a remarkable period of my life. I am grateful to Editor Heidi Greco for helping me to this end.

To my husband, I wish to express my fervent appreciation for his humour, sincerity and his unyielding encouragement of my finest efforts.

To my children, I wish to thank them for these cherished years without which my life would truly lack meaning. It is an honour to be their Mother.

And to my parents, without their steadying influence, their confidence in my abilities and their heartened support all through my life none of this could have come to fruition.

RIPPLES

As time speeds past like lightning in an incandescent sky
I spy the fingerprints upon my wall.
I know a time will come when they will vanish from my home
But I'll see them when the shadows fall.

Arriving here is bittersweet but I'm compelled to tell
Of fleeting years with looming shore espied.
I offer signposts for your course, a glimpse of possibilities
For you to consider or deny.

For I know that as each ripple lands upon a page
A new wave is created and sent forth.
Each family sways with different swells, with different points of view,
Creating dreams by trying many oars.

INTRODUCTION

Regardless of the classification that is assigned to this book—memoir, treatise, compilation, guidebook or something else entirely—*To the Shore of a Child's Ocean, Part One* is a sincere portrayal of one of the most enlightening yet challenging decades of my life. Over these fleeting, precious years, I have marvelled at the gift bestowed upon me by my children: the role of mother. For that, I am ever thankful.

Early on in our homeschooling journey, I established myself as a contact person for our greater homeschooling community, volunteering my time and energy. Over the years, I have spoken to countless individuals who were in need of direction and counsel on their voyage and others who were considering homeschooling and required concrete fundamentals. I eventually came to the realization that a void exists in Canadian homeschooling resources and literature. I felt that further dialogue was necessary to advance the promotion of quality in both parenting and education.

With this book, I hope to offer parents, especially new parents, a sense of optimism and a glimpse of possibilities. *To the Shore of a Child's Ocean, Part One* is the first instalment of the story of one Canadian family's journey in the dynamic educational culture that is homeschooling.

CHAPTER ONE—THE SOURCE

Anxiously staring out of our fingerprint-smudged front window, I exhale forcibly in a futile attempt to expel my buzzing case of nerves. The children squeal in animated delight as their adrenaline practically oozes onto the living room carpet. We are awaiting the arrival of a visitor from my past. Although my memory of her has been dulled with time, she has remained steadfast in my heart. Julia. She is a friend from a long-ago time of mystery, future and adolescent tortures—I mean…fortunes.

I'd received the phone call late last week, and it had left me in a state of shock and agitation. My friend from a confused land called high school was coming for a long overdue visit; this would be the first time I'd see her in almost ten years. A good friend yes, but changes had taken place and time had led each of us in clearly different directions.

Julia had quite literally married the man next door, moved merrily to Canada's oil patch in southern Alberta, and embarked on an odyssey through perpetual suburbia. Her life was complete, with two children— one of each kind, and no shedding pets.

I, on the other hand, had escaped my prairie upbringing and moved to the beautiful west coast of Canada with my future husband. Within a year, we were married and overnight (it seemed like it anyway), found ourselves the parents of two rascally children. Did I mention we also had a deeply loved but heavily shedding dog?

Aside from the dog, you may think that Julia and I had reasonably comparable lifestyles, but you'd be missing one vital difference. My husband and I made the decision to homeschool our children.

Julia and I had shared our developing years near a small prairie town, surrounded by mile upon mile of planted crops and often grey sky and bush. I'd met Julia during the first month of high school at a dance at the local curling rink/ballroom.

Even though it was only September, crisp snow was already on the ground. As I skidded my way to my 1980s vintage red sports car after a fun-filled evening, Maureen, a girl of average build, medium hair and standard attitude, beckoned to me from her 1980s vintage red pickup. I made my way to the passenger side of the truck, aiming to hide my awkwardness and trying my best to present an image of self-control and mature aloofness.

Maureen squealed, "Hi!" and introduced Julia, a slim, ash-blonde girl with square, gleaming teeth and smooth, round cheeks. As Maureen presented her completely unique view of the evening, Julia and I laughed, continually glancing around at oblivious passersby. We hoped that our efforts at portraying coolness and composure were being noticed and after another 20 minutes or so of pleasantries and juvenile banter, I continued the slipping slide to my car, where I was thankful to turn up the heat while I headed home rehashing the evening and berating myself over things I had said, imagining them all to be completely idiotic.

The following Monday arrived too soon and a blaring horn brought me to my senses and into undignified action. Armed with my pile of enchanting, mostly mind-numbing textbooks, I raced less than gracefully to the putrid yellow school bus already edging its way out of our yard and managed to arrive at its door as it finally came to a halt. I climbed the stairs and found a seat at the very back, totally out of breath and shaking my head in utter disgust and loathing.

This decaying yellow behemoth was driven by the hardest woman I ever knew, and I'd taken it every day for ten long years. Lurching and rolling in a state of controlled rebellion, we arrived at our destination with five minutes to spare before classes commenced.

We teenagers exited the agonizing misery of a bus and made our way inside to waiting hallway benches where we met other herded students and discussed the past weekend's dance and its inescapable mishaps. Julia and I recognized each other at opposite sides of the same bench and struck up a conversation. As we laughed at the same ridiculous events of the weekend, our guards came down and before long any feelings of unease and insecurity dissipated. On that day, the seed of our friendship was planted and it carried us all through high school.

As you can see, my high school experience, had all the grace, charm and beauty of a hairless dog. The teachers seemed to hurry through our lessons, leaving no time for questions. We took what we could from them and didn't worry about the rest. I managed to squeak out an A average and upon graduation, paused to thank one teacher. Julia fared as well and armed with our diplomas, we headed off to city lights, to university and to an unknown future.

Roommates at university, Julia and I tackled a new city, friends both new and old, and a growing ideological distance. As I gaze out the window anticipating her imminent arrival, I cannot help but wonder how we got to this somewhat disconnected place, friends yet virtual strangers.

After convocation, we traveled down different forks in the road but still managed to keep in touch—first with phone calls on our birthdays, later with cards that arrived late and now the sporadic email. But what has remained through these fragmented years is that familiar confluence, that awareness of a genuine bond between us that transcends the gulf of our divergent lives.

The door to our friendship had been reopened by an email from Julia, some six months earlier. Although it seemed innocuous, it had shown me just how dissimilar our lives had become.

Chris,

How are things? Things are good here. The kids have been busy at school and we have taken in a live-in nanny to look after them after school and on weekends. Mike is still working for the oil refinery and hopes to take some time off in April. We plan to go to Los Angeles!— cannot wait! The kids are upset that they cannot go but Olivia (the nanny) will stay with them. We are in the process of buying a cottage at a local ski hill. It would be great if you two came for a visit and we spent some time up there.

Anyway, hope all is well,

Julia

CHAPTER TWO—CURRENTS

We chose to homeschool our children. This is an exceedingly straight-forward statement but it serves as a beacon marking the difference between those who choose to homeschool and those who do not.

What is it that creates this apparent need in some families but not in others? This question filled my mind as I waited for Julia to arrive in our driveway. Given our very similar backgrounds, education and experiences, how had she and I developed into such different individuals?

Waiting by that window, I took a hard look at who I had become. I'd been existing in what felt like a perpetual purgatory until I met my future husband in 1991. I felt as if I'd been waiting for him, somewhat impatiently, my whole long life. And I knew him instantly and completely the moment I laid eyes on him. I immediately believed that he was the partner I was always meant to have and I wanted to get on with the business of our life together.

Never feeling like I fully integrated meaningfully with my peers or my community, I had begun to view my life as a fundamental misplacement. Aside from Julia, I hadn't had a lot of deep friendships in high school or university. I was reasonably well-liked, but I always had the feeling I was somewhat out of place. Adding to this, I was planted in the middle of a country so vast it could make your head spin and I felt that simple, homogeneous prairie life had nothing to offer me and I longed for diversity and the atypical.

I was raised on a working farm with chores to do, manure to experience close up and personal, and weather to encounter with fierceness. But as severe as it could be at times, it was also straightforward and honourable. It was my home and served as my symbol of durability. I was safe there and felt its permanence even at a very young age.

My father was a pioneer, breaking sod since he could walk and the meaning of life for him was found in perseverance and fortitude. Depth had more to do with topsoil than something profound, and fancy meant a new tractor. He had an acceptance of his lot in life from his earliest childhood and felt he truly belonged to the land.

As for my mother, you could say she was—well...experienced. Born in the 1930s in Berlin, Germany, my mother met tragedy and ruin face to face at the hands of the Nazis and the Gestapo. Life simply meant survival for another day and hope was pushed into the corners of bunkers and cellars. Battered and torn, my mother emerged from the debris, a woman of undying strength, forever changed but ultimately enduring. Fleeing to Canada after the war, she encountered a land as different from post-war Europe as Venus. Vast and wild, safe and growing, Canada offered my mother a refuge and a dream. Armed with her keen resourcefulness, she embraced her new life, worked hard and in due course married twice, mothered three children and remains eternally thankful for each and every day.

My upbringing was steadfastly rooted by these two individuals. I never arrived home to an empty house, food was healthful, real and I knew where it came from, and we laboured vigorously to contribute something to the farm. They gave me an uncomplicated upbringing ingrained with honesty, forthrightness and stability fuelled by their assiduous parental love.

Julia's story is a familiar one. Her parents were both from small towns on the prairie, linked to the land by the wind and the wheat. Her mother worked as a bank teller for 40-odd years—- filling out forms, counting out cash and handing out the occasional disapproving look to those she deemed irresponsible. Her father owned the local hardware store and never missed a day of work. Her parents promoted a home life that encouraged Julia and her siblings to develop straight and sound. Above all else, they had an affinity for the prudent and practical and sought quiet, sensible lives fraught with as little of the undefined as possible. Roots were indeed, firmly planted.

Our families were not outwardly dissimilar. Home life in each offered security that was both consistent and responsible, and prairie dependability encircled us all in a blanket of eternal constancy. So what could account for the markedly different lifestyles the offspring of these families chose? What specific gifts did my parents bestow upon me that promoted my unconventional nature?

I experienced an epiphany when I recalled a meeting I'd had preceding my imminent graduation from high school. I was having difficulty deciding what field of study to pursue at university so I set up an afternoon appointment with the high school guidance counsellor.

He was an emaciated mouse of a man with a thin moustache and, if possible, even thinner skin. I was to list three occupations I considered compatible with my interests and present them at our upcoming meeting. I decided at the last minute to invite my mother to the meeting and as we sat in his dark hovel of an office, five minutes before my appointment, I felt disconcertingly murky and as out of focus as the room. I had no idea where this meeting would ultimately lead and was anxious for it to be over so I could return to my familiar, albeit befuddled life.

Precisely on time, the counsellor scurried in, his rumpled three-piece suit as ill-fitting as his expression when he discovered the presence of a parent in his office. He took an audible deep breath and asked in a shaky voice as to how the exercise had gone. My mother, enthusiastically—and I, reluctantly—handed him our papers in absolute silence.

He proceeded to gingerly unfold my stained and tattered paper as if it was the repugnant stomach lining of a goat, and then turned it over—once, twice. His smile never reached his undersized, pig-like eyes. At first, he did not seem to appreciate the fact that I had not written anything on the paper. He then ventured to assure me, condescendingly, that this was, "a normal occurrence for someone my age and was perfectly understandable under the circumstances." Shifting uneasily in his antiquated, maroon vinyl chair, he fearfully commenced the unfolding of my mother's neatly typed offering.

Upon reading the words on her paper, his expression, shall we say, changed. He looked as if he were about to commit a double murder right there in his office and I shrank back in bewildered panic. My mother steadied her gaze, and I made to hide behind her skirt like a child facing her worst nightmare. He gathered various manuals and questionnaires and practically hurled them in my direction, pausing only to wish us a brutally harsh, "Good Day!"

As we launched ourselves into the car, I glared at my mother in horror and demanded an explanation. Barely managing to maintain control of the Le Baron as she accelerated out of the parking lot, she exploded with exasperation, "Deep Sea Diver!" My mouth dropped in pure astonishment; I sat quietly for a moment, pondering what had just occurred, trying to unravel the mystery of his extreme reaction to my mother's contribution.

And then it came to me. My mother's response to his inquiry was completely consistent with her personal views on pursuing a fulfilled life. Her life had taught her that anything was possible and you should only be limited in your pursuits by your imagination, ability to work hard and your resolve. She was very simply trying to promote vigorous dialogue and honest exploration of options, with no intention of creating an atmosphere of disparagement and defensiveness. The counsellor must have believed he was being hoodwinked by my mother's apparently unreasonable response and felt it necessary to plunge into combat mode.

Not only was I raised with **roots**, secure in the knowledge that my internal foundation, my core was sound and deep-rooted but I had always been strongly encouraged (much more than many of my peers were) to take the next step, to **reach** for the prize, to question standard thinking and to appreciate that risk meant a richer life. I was supported in my sometimes discouraging efforts to think outside the box before I painted myself into a corner. I remember my mother frequently reciting the old adage, "Reach for the stars! If you fail, you just might land on the moon".

Being told that I could do anything that I set my sights on afforded me the freedom to try and keep trying because I knew I could safely withdraw at anytime. My groundwork had been well constructed and my sense of home was fixed firmly in place. I had full knowledge that when I needed to retreat and lick my wounds, I had a soft, sympathetic cushion available to me to bolster my fortitude and prop me up for the next round.

When I encountered difficulties, I was often left to my own devises until such a time as I asked my parents for help. They wished to respect my autonomy, my own capabilities and resourcefulness, my **reason** and were only prepared to help when I requested it. When I did ask, I was met with complete cooperation and a joint concerted effort toward helping me achieve my own potential.

I felt a keen sense that I was loved unconditionally, nurtured with a respect for who I was and who I would become. I felt safe to grow and take chances because they were my chances to take and my choices were accepted by my parents, regardless of their own particular views or sensibilities, because they were my choices to make.

These three gifts:

- **Roots:** a genuine sense of security, total stability and inner strength,

- **Reach:** a desire to pursue aspirations, an ability to imagine alternatives and the capacity to dream,

- **Reason:** confidence in my capability, resourcefulness and competence,

lent buoyancy to my strong commitment to question prevailing norms, heartened my unconventional nature and helped promote my openness to alternatives. Without these gifts, my efforts to reach beyond existing limits and succeed would certainly have been hindered if not completely thwarted, rendering me a markedly changed person.

Once we finally arrived at home, frazzled but unharmed, I tentatively flipped through the heap of literature he had unloaded on me. In its midst was a seemingly exhaustive list of potential occupations compiled by the school board. It was presented in a strict, authoritative manner clearly designed to communicate its all-inclusive yet practical merits. Strange at it might seem, Deep Sea Diver was not even mentioned. Apparently, those individuals graduating within my high school's land locked prairie catchment area need not consider diving as a viable occupation let alone pursuit of study.

BUT WHAT ABOUT my own personal school experience? Was it really so appalling that I would never even consider sending my own children to a traditional institution of learning? I turned out well-adjusted and contributing to society—why not give my children roots, reach and reason within my home and then send them off to school to receive further tools to help them along their life journey?

The best way to explain this dilemma may again be with an illustration from my past. When I was seven, I was placed in a large class at the local elementary school. There were more than 40 of us in there, with just as many little voices to be heard and issues to be resolved. Our teacher as I remember, maintained reasonable control of the classroom and at times we even managed to have structured "fun".

Every week, we participated in the traditional "show and tell", an exercise where each student would bring an object from home to present to the rest of the class. We all eagerly anticipated this assignment as it was a respite from the rest of our mostly colourless weekly routine.

One week our teacher changed the format of this exercise to "show and tell about a parent". We were to present one of our parents to the class and provide details as to what activities that parent was occupied with during an average day. In retrospect, I suppose it was short-sightedness on the part of the teacher because on the following Thursday, 46 children presented their 46 mothers, and each related virtually identical stories!

These parents were all mothers who chose to stay at home. They made beds, cooked meals, cleaned up after the dog/cat/hamster and provided a home for their family. In Canada, the early 1970s were a time when it was still common for one parent to remain in the home, taking full-time responsibility for the children while the other parent served as the "bread-winner", working outside the home in some capacity to pay for the necessities of life. Children were dispatched to school by the age of six to receive an education like expectant, empty slates. If a child was fortunate, they were set off into adulthood in possession of deep roots, strong reach and adept reasoning abilities facilitated by their parents and their school in conjunction. It was not, however, an era of home-schooling.

WITH THE PREVIOUS generation, it was not only monetarily feasible but socially coveted for one parent to remain in the home to maintain a stable home environment for the family. Today however, static wages have made it next to impossible in many cases for the "bread winner" to keep up with rising inflation and the increased demands of rampant consumerism. At the same time, the women's movement has forged new (and long overdue) inroads into the male-dominated workplace.

As a result of these events and others, a new collective mentality in western society has been created, altering nuclear family dynamics.

It has become a seemingly obligatory way of life in many households for both adult members of the family to work full-time outside the home. Participation in career advancement at the expense of both personal life and family is also becoming the norm. This dedication to your workplace results in an increasingly healthy bottom-line—at least for employers. Our society has come to rely on the benefits of the expanded labour force and families as a whole often feel they can no longer survive without the added income generated by having both parents working.

Stagnant wages, mounting consumerism, the devaluation of home-making skills, as well as the notion of happiness based on career accomplishment—all of these have contributed to society's unfolding problem—who is going to take care of the children? As a result, daycares have been established everywhere, school is being promoted earlier, and preschools have become the norm. Today's government mantra seems to be the sooner we can move our children from the home and into the care-giving system, the better for all. But what kind of influence has this had on children?

Regularly, by six months of age, children are placed in a daycare environment so that both parents can return to the work force. Consequently, guidance is being supplied to many of society's children by persons who do not sincerely love them and are qualified to care for them only by the issuance of certificates. To add to this, children end up spending most of their days with caregivers who are unfortunately, often overworked and impatient.

Many children are not only being stripped of a committed relationship with their parents and being forced to rely on others, but are being denied important aspects of their childhood. By age three many more children are placed in preschool with the promise that early introduction of educational concepts begets future triumph. Parlance of these times is that the earlier children enter the educational (and some say the political-economic) system, the better. Such beliefs have become another way of convincing parents that they are performing an act of propriety by sending their children to school as early as possible—to prepare their children with a "head start" to their future schooling. It also reinforces the notion that they are being responsible by getting back to the business of work.

Free, unstructured play-time for these children is often perceived as a misuse of a child's time and is set at a minimum. A structured, academic-laden day is seen to meld nicely to the demands of future schooling. Unfortunately, by the time children reach "school age", many children no longer remember how to play or think independently or creatively. They have been scheduled, often to the point of manic dependence and their childhood has been greatly disrupted. This rigid scheduling evident in many preschool environments seems designed to thwart both creative and independent thought and the extra effort seemingly required to manage each of these. But what has actually been created is a more exhausting work environment for teachers due to myriad behavioural problems.

To a large extent, much of traditional education has been adjourned as teachers scramble to accommodate behavioural issues unheard of in schools of the past. With the absence of strong family ties, disparate student-teacher ratios and often a child's inability to think independently, the role of peers has grown so much that rules of behaviour, however inappropriate, are often dictated by them. Teachers have become substitute parents and counsellors, doing their best to provide guidance to children who have been on their own emotionally for as long as they can remember. Teachers, who have always accepted the responsibility for educating society's children, are now becoming overwhelmed by a work environment fraught with behavioural concerns and the need to impart so many of the basics that parents once provided. Not even their deeply-rooted educational pillars of reading, writing and arithmetic are always being met as they struggle to maintain control of the classroom.

Following these increasingly structured days, children often return home from school to an empty house where they will microwave a pre-packaged meal, watch hours of mindless television, become awash in the virtual world provided by computers or be practically imprisoned in their rooms with a glut of homework. If, miraculously, an adult is present, they will often spend their time driving their children to countless extra-curricular activities designed not so much to promote the children's abilities and health as to simply keep them occupied. Little time is salvaged for family, little time is conserved for childhood, and as a result, little time is left for the requisite planting of **roots**, encouragement of **reach** and the nurturing of **reason**.

And as for that professed "head start" into the world of education, studies have shown that children who attend preschool are no further advanced in scholarship and reason. In fact, when you consider their levels of creativity and original thought, they are losing ground. As we know, children hold the future in their hands. I believe that, without the ability to be creative and to think independently, our culture will languish.

I realize that I have presented a rather bleak depiction of today's western society and its educational system. With careful appreciation for the slipperiness of generalizations, I maintain that the statements I have presented serve to illustrate the fundamental course our society is taking. We place far too much emphasis on pursuing **the** alleged good life at the expense of living **a** truly good life.

Many of today's children are being bilked of the basics for future personal fulfillment that parents and schools once nurtured. I believe that parents must take responsibility for ensuring that their children are provided with what I consider the original three R's—**roots**, **reach** and **reason**.

WITH THIS KIND of firm foundation, children are better equipped to discover their own independent meaning of success with confidence. With the many problems inherent in western society and in schools today, the decision to homeschool is an increasingly attractive notion. However, without the support and encouragement of my husband, I am convinced that maintaining my current level of commitment to this journey would be much more challenging, if not impossible.

My husband and I had escaped the windblown prairies, (he feeling misplaced as well) New Years Day, 1996. We landed on Vancouver Island, a place we thought of as "our island", feeling fresh, revitalized and invincible. The heavy rain clouds parted miraculously as we drove off the ferry into a land of cherry blossoms, gentle ocean breezes and possibilities. Everything suddenly felt achievable. As opportunities presented themselves, my husband started his own consulting company and I continued my career in finance. We felt that we were in control of our destiny as in no other time in our lives together. And then we got pregnant. So much for feeling in control of our fate! We were complete-ly, yet happily stunned. Reflecting on it today, we laugh at our absolute bafflement as in reality, it was a hugely passive stage compared with the many challenges of parenthood.

When I first tentatively considered homeschooling I was vastly preg-nant with my first child. I was grappling with all the frightening unknowns a parent-to-be experiences when faced with the coming event, only I had the added blessing of realizing that I'd never even held a baby before! The future was an unknown, foreign place. Like so many couples before us, we had not consciously set out to begin a family. The preg-nancy felt like the intervention of Providence. She took us by the hand and we had no choice but to relinquish all power to her process. We were clinging to her and each other as we faced the countless ques-tions we knew a life raising children would ask of us.

My parents had provided me with a firm grounding in family, con-fidence in my abilities and a strong desire to reach beyond prevailing norms. By always respecting my decisions and gently encouraging pos-sibility, my parents allowed me to discover my own path. My husband and I, both independent-minded individuals, considered the innumer-able benefits of homeschooling and decided they would completely outweigh any disadvantages of the loss of one income. My husband and I take parenting very seriously and truly regard homeschooling as the only logical choice for our family. With his love and support I feel that we can all authentically prosper.

CHAPTER THREE—THE RIVER BED

The birth of our daughter in January, 1997, ushered in a year of resplendent parenthood and we delighted in our lot. Before long we were pregnant again and in October, 1998 our son arrived and our family felt idyllically whole.

Like many parents who choose to homeschool their children, I sought to ensure there would be no separation between life and education. I embarked on our homeschooling journey the moment each of our children arrived by spending time playing with them, reading to them and looking after their basic needs. It was a beautiful, liberating time that I savoured as it filled my soul with tender purpose. I attended to their every meal, their every whim and their every diaper change. I was beholden to no others but my own immediate family and witnessed each phase and each accomplishment with awareness of my growing love and good fortune.

An indispensable aspect of this time lay in the way it allowed us to establish our own personal goals for homeschooling our children. As a homeschooling parent, I believe you must take time to consider what it is you ultimately desire for your children. What follows is a list of central issues we considered in our pursuit of an educational proposal for homeschooling our children. It is a process that has evolved and been transformed into a lifestyle.

Central Issues

- We wanted to ensure that the teaching methods utilized were not just suitable but custom-made for our children's individual personalities and capabilities. We wanted to provide a personalized learning plan for each of our children based on their interests and aptitudes and limited only by our collective imagination and determination.
- We demanded a learning environment that would be devoid of negative social behaviours such as bullying, harassment and discrimination.

- We wanted our children to experience the benefits of a flexible learning environment where they would be encouraged to pursue their own interests and would be exposed to new and stimulating ideas and things. We longed for an atmosphere that was free of strained instruction and controlled curricula and hoped to infuse their imagination with wonder.
- We aspired to ensure that our children had ample time to absorb their surroundings and to savour the precious years of their childhood.
- We believed it was essential for our family to remain a close and cohesive unit, with all members sharing a concrete awareness of belonging and contributing to the family entity. We wanted to meet our responsibilities as parents head-on and foster strong family ties and well-being.
- We longed for an education experience for our children that rejected the undue influence of peer pressure and lemming mentality. We hoped to instill in our children the self-confidence necessary to override any untoward manipulation from their friends or associates.
- We wanted our children to mature in an environment free of explicit labelling and departmentalization based on age or other preconceived perceptions and artificial limitations.
- We sought an educational climate that would expose our children to authenticity, real-life experience and genuine, unaffected relationships.
- We wished to ensure that impediments and obstacles to learning were minimized. We hoped to provide our children with individualized, one-on-one attention and guidance free from unreasonable delays and diversions.
- We hoped to instill a genuine love of learning in our children. We planned to do this by giving them unfaltering encouragement as they made their quest to become lifelong learners and seekers.

As a direct result of working my way through these considerations, I formulated my raison d'être. My ambition was to ensure that my children were grounded by a firm planting in family—**roots**, and that they would develop a keen sense of belonging which would lead them to active participation in our family unit. I wished for them to have the confidence to tackle life's unknowns and recognize that their only limitations were the strength of their determination and their ability to dream—**reach**.

Lastly, I wanted them to have the ability and self-assurance necessary to **reason** through their world and face their future with proficiency.

By providing them with these basics, I felt I was not only fulfilling my responsibility as a parent but also laying the groundwork for their future independent successes. By equipping them with these fundamentals, I hoped the children would discover their own genuine meanings of success and learn to rely on their own resources to prevail as independent beings. Ultimately, I hoped to foster my children's capacity for discovery and a commitment to pursue their own deepest instincts so they might achieve the greatest happiness in their quest for **a** good life.

WHEN YOUR BASIC ambitions have been established, I believe it is vital to become more specific regarding your personal philosophy of homeschooling. Reading through countless books and testimonials at the library and the bookstores, viewing the various websites devoted to homeschooling and other educational options, and establishing contact with veteran homeschoolers are perhaps the best routes to take. Although it can become quite overwhelming, I am convinced this research is completely indispensable to adequately realize your objectives. You should become aware of the options available, and then narrow down your search to those ideas that seem most beneficial to your own personal homeschooling beliefs.

The following presents a brief summary of key principles in the most frequently utilized homeschooling philosophies to date.

Homeschooling Philosophies

- Families new to homeschooling often presume that they will actively teach their children with periodic grading and tests, with a packaged curriculum and comprehensive textbooks and will manage their children's education precisely as schools have done in the past. They consider their children as vessels waiting to be filled or slates in need of words. This philosophy, known as **School at Home or Traditional** Homeschooling works well for those families who embrace a more conventional approach to most matters.

- A more moderate method is **Unit Study** Homeschooling. Families adopting this option choose a main topic for a given year in accordance with their children's interests or experiences and integrate this as a specific theme around which to study various subjects or concepts. For example, a family may choose spiders as a topic for exploration: for science, they might examine its body parts and how it lives; for geography, they might consider where various species are found, etc.

- One popular approach to homeschooling is based on theories and techniques developed by **Charlotte Mason**, a 19th century educator. She suggested that children should to be trained in the practice of narration, in other words, storytelling. Mason emphasized the importance of considering what children *do* rather than what they do not know. She also promoted the benefits of classic literature and noble poetry, believing that children should be offered the best books, music and art. To put it concisely, she believed that children should be raised in the realm of the humanities.

- **Waldorf Inspired** Homeschooling is based on teachings of Rudolph Steiner, an educator of the late 19th and early 20th centuries. With his philosophy, intelligence is regarded not merely as a manifestation of the mind but as an integral part of an individual's spirit as well. This perspective encourages development of a child's imagination, creativity and fantasy life. It promotes the view that children learn best through "heart energy" or love. The love of learning is encouraged by gently cultivating and imparting meaning through incorporating the intellectual, physical and spiritual elements of life at various stages of a child's development.

- Basic literacy and numeracy, coupled with Latin, Greek and higher order thinking skills are harmonized when a parent applies a **Classical or Trivium** method to homeschooling. The nucleus of Classical Education is the trivium which serves as a teaching model that undertakes to match the curriculum to a child's cognitive development. Concrete, analytical and abstract thinking are exposed at various stages of a child's development, along with Grammar, Dialectic and Rhetoric—subjects introduced to help accomplish the goals of the trivium.

- Perhaps the most controversial approach to homeschooling education is **Natural** or **Child-led Learning**. It is often referred to as **Unschooling**. It is based on the principle that children can and will take command of their own education. With this model, the parent's role is altered to that of facilitator rather than teacher. Education becomes likened to the kindling of a flame rather than the filling of a vessel, as a child's interests and curiosities dictate the direction of learning. In turn, these pursuits are promoted with support from the parents. Learning is viewed as a fluid experience that may occur anywhere and at any time, united intrinsically with daily life.

- By far the most frequently applied method of homeschooling is **Eclectic Homeschooling**. This method covers any combination of the aforementioned designs as well as any other proposals deemed appropriate. With the mixing and matching of philosophies and the merging of the parent's personality with the child's learning styles, a unique approach can be created, one that is best suited to the particular learner. This method allows a parent to establish a learning environment committed to the singular spirit of their child, an environment limited only by a parent's imagination and inspiration. This methodology stems from confidence in the tenet that no one knows a child better than his or her own parents.

ONCE THE FOUNDATION has been laid for your fundamental philosophy, many homeschooling parents enter a stage of rosy optimism and misplaced expectation. September often arrives with homeschooling families blushing with obvious enthusiasm, ready to apply their well-researched strategies on their unsuspecting children. Reality, however, often takes a bite out of those plans and spits out a much transformed arrangement. And there lies a well-learned lesson of homeschooling that I can personally vouch for: **Be flexible**.

Homeschooling is a dynamic, ever-changing process and I feel it is worthwhile for a parent to be adaptable and willing to explore the innumerable array of resources that are at your disposal. Children benefit significantly from a parent's abandonment of impractical demands. By setting aside unworkable strategies, a parent shows respect and empathy to their children rather than leaving them with feelings of failure, disappointment or frustration. This leads to confidence which grows out of these positive experiences. Such willingness to adjust offers support to a child's homeschooling passage.

Regardless of the many homeschooling books, websites and magazines available, I have discovered that when utterly confused, frustrated or overwhelmed with the inevitable challenges of homeschooling, the finest course of action is often to let your heart lead the way. Children learn exceptionally well within the arms of a parent's love and when it comes right down to it, that is all that they really want. By being present for them, a parent gives buoyancy to a child's belief system and strengthens their life bond. The strongest lever in a homeschooling parent's toolkit is a deep understanding of their children and a firm belief in them. This awareness coupled with a strong relationship, lays the foundation for the best education a child can receive. With knowledge of a child's inner workings, a parent learns to instinctively provide what is best for that child's individual needs.

AS I WADED through my research, I began to develop a partiality for Waldorf Inspired Homeschooling. I appreciated the Waldorf notion that a child's greatest gift is not their intellect but their imagination, and that an individual's core capacity is achieved only when there is a convergence of the physical (the will realm—dominant up to approximately age seven), the spiritual (the feeling realm—dominant up to approximately age 14) and the intellectual (the thinking realm—awakened at approximately age 15).

The Natural or Child-Led Homeschooling philosophy also offered many views that appealed to me. Established primarily in the 1960s by John Holt, it is a perspective that embraces the child, unconditionally and wholly, and considers a child's imagination and creativity to be essential to their happiness. I particularly appreciated his "unschooling" approach of encouraging free exploration with unmitigated trust and respect. By allowing children to follow their passions and curiosities, a parent bestows confidence. By valuing their children's decisions, they contribute greatly to their child's pursuit of a rewarding life experience. The concept of all of life being in concert with true education resonated with my need for the seamless blending of learning with daily life experience.

When considering what type of books to enlist in my homeschooling approach, I tended to value "real" books, similar to a Charlotte Mason/Waldorf Inspired design. By "real" I mean I preferred books with a transcendent life lesson, beautifully crafted with imaginative thought. Books chosen tended to articulate meaning in a style that a child could fully take possession of and embrace. The mere divulging of plot or facts was insufficient to fully surmount the page or to inspire further dialogue or significance. Many of the books in our home library were capable of transporting you to a magical domain and served to inform with fervour rather than with lifeless printed words.

It has been my experience that explicitly teaching and constant testing have elements of hypocrisy and faithlessness. They are frequently manifested slyly and demonstrate a marked distrust in a child's ability. I much prefer an approach based on confidence and recognition of a child's resourcefulness and ability to form connections. By supplementing a child's travels with engaging ideas, discoveries and concepts, moments of curiosity are habitually sparked promoting self-education, a much more powerful teacher than static pronouncements of fact. I feel it is the spirit of awakening inherent genius not the imposition of lifeless techniques and devices that most benefit a child's burgeoning intellectual capacity.

An elemental aspect and obvious benefit of homeschooling lies in its ongoing engagement with the world. When there is no separation between daily life and education, learning and living transpire concurrently with connections becoming internalized more efficiently as a result. There is always enough time to attain true understanding because learning becomes just another aspect of life, as natural as eating or breathing. I have found that this lack of separation between education and everyday life creates a true love of learning, one that will lead to a lifelong habit of curiosity. With such awareness comes contentment and a consciousness of reality that transcends attitudes promoted by traditional education.

In so many institutions of traditional learning, rote learning and standardized tests have taken such priority over discovery that it is astounding inventiveness can endure. It is my contention that if our society is to advance, we can never encourage acceptance of codes or obedience to norms without examining them and questioning their validity. A parent's ability to actively listen and encourage does more to support a child grappling with their own analysis of their world than any test or examination ever will. True education arrives in knowledge that is earned through internalized experience not in what you are spoon-fed.

I believe that parents have the utmost responsibility to provide their children with a childhood, to permit them to be children before these most cherished years vanish forever. Because I believe that a child's greatest strength lies not in their logical intellect but in their imagination, I feel that this gift must be encouraged and nourished accordingly. Children utilize fantasy and dreams—not to escape their world, but to better appreciate it. Parents have a duty to support their children's sense of wonder and encourage their ability to dream and be childish.

Another essential truth that I have discovered on my homeschooling voyage is the value of a parent's own self-nurturing. A parent who regularly sets aside time to pursue personal passions and indulgences remains better focused and is more capable when coping with the daily challenges of homeschooling. You must be diligent in getting enough rest and allowing enough time to listen to your own inner voice. Treating yourself now and then not only benefits the parent involved but the entire family. Children especially need to witness a parent's pursuit of self-fulfillment. It will help them to better appreciate a parent as an individual with their own identity and dreams. Further, it will help develop an image of themselves as adults. A parent is the greatest role model a child will ever have and it is vital that a family not get mired in detail and schedules misplacing their own life's delight. Tomorrow is never promised and it is crucial that you live as consciously as possible and remain aware that each moment is a gift. Dispatching this awareness to a child is of utmost importance to their growing self-actualization and well-being.

My approach to homeschooling falls into the category of Eclectic Homeschooling. I have implemented my design using many ingredients from the prevailing methodologies but have discarded those that do not mesh well with our family's beliefs, our love and our spirit. I have created an approach that aims to embrace my children's interests and individuality while inviting beauty and wonder to their days. I tend the flame of their creativity in a warm, secure environment as we prepare together for their future. I seek to facilitate my children's journey in a gentle, respectful, and patient manner to ensure they will be capable of attaining their greatest happiness. I aim to provide inspiration and discovery along the path to their ocean and celebrate their reach for tomorrow.

CHAPTER FOUR—UP TO AGE FIVE

Nautical Compass—Up To Age Five

I began my homeschooling journey virtually the moment my children were born. Natural and instinctive, it was a loving endeavour that filled our days with warmth and impetuous energy. Unconditional love, active participation and conscious parenting provided days that were uncomplicated, unaffected and gratifying. Our emphasis on spontaneity and imagination provided the children with many happy learning opportunities and encouraged them to express their innate capabilities.

I believe that true education means recognizing the authentic meaning behind everything we're exposed to. With this in mind, it follows that true knowledge begins at home with practical experience in daily life. Up until about age seven, children generally learn best through imitation and active manipulation of objects—they are habitants of the will realm. These early simulations and experiences should be encouraged wholeheartedly. Children not only enjoy life more by participating in it than by having it simply take place around them, but these activities promote a confidence in and richer understanding of the inter-relationships between events. Although minding young children while trying to prepare a nutritious meal can be a challenge, when children feel genuinely welcomed and encouraged in helping with such tasks, they can contribute significantly. The result is that we all benefit greatly from the experience.

Being active participants in the day-to-day family home is an important life skill that cannot be pioneered too early. When participation is promoted and is acknowledged by a sincere appreciation of effort, children not only gain useful skills, but they develop a better awareness of family dynamics and learn a genuine respect for home and for each member of the family. Involvement in daily household tasks and playing an active role in the ordinary rhythms of the day contribute to a child's sense of belonging, which in turn promotes self-assurance and confidence in their abilities.

Imitation of a parent is probably the basis of every child's quickest and most straightforward lessons. Children will rarely misquote a parent. As many can attest, they are known to brilliantly repeat word-for-word what their parents have said, regardless of propriety! This is only one of the reasons it is so essential always to strive to act in a way that is worthy of imitation. It follows, therefore, that when children witness a parent's active participation in the quest for knowledge and new experiences they will be more apt to model these behaviours as well.

Because I wanted my children to be free from undue restrictions in their learning endeavours and strove to ensure their education would progress in a more natural fashion, I avoided rigorous instruction and resisted my innate urge to rescue them when their discoveries led to frustration. Instead, we pursued the natural patterns of our days with energetic activities followed by time for rest, the unrestrained followed by measured steps, rising and falling like waves throughout each day. In short, we respected the rhythm of our heartbeats. As a result, the children were emancipated in their play with few interruptions as they pursued their interests.

Very young children experience their surroundings through movement and hands on manipulation. Parents need to be aware of this and not only accept their child's needs but encourage the manifestation of them. While every parent hopes that their children will act resolutely and resourcefully, such sturdiness of character can only be promoted by acknowledging and supporting a child's natural tendencies.

BECAUSE OUR HOME was our "classroom", we ensured that it was always suitably stocked with a range of high-quality materials and appealing supplies. Our stocks included dress-up clothes and old jewellery, clay and beeswax, various types and textures of paper, an abundance of art supplies and natural items like seashells, stones, nuts, and pine cones. These were always readily available and easily accessible for spontaneous creative outbursts. Artistic explosions were supported and limited only by our imagination. Assistance was provided only when solicited. With each handful of sparkle and dollop of glue that decorated nearly every lopsided, sticky creation, the children truly owned their artwork and felt great pride in their efforts. This was very important and helped them develop confidence in their creative endeavours and subsequent feelings of self-worth.

We manipulated play dough to give structure to personal inclinations and experimented with primary colours to delight the senses. We enjoyed using the finest materials available and practiced freedom of expression in the extreme. My participation as an equal partner allowed me to experience tangible joy from my own creations and I happily welcomed childish artistic exuberance back into my adult world.

Living on the wild, yet mild, west coast of Canada enabled year-round exploration of the numerous beaches, hiking trails and forested parks near our home. The natural world served to extend and enrich our home "classroom", and we spent a wealth of time unearthing and considering its many wonders. Often we would arrive home buoyant, armed with baskets of natural objects and interesting miscellany. We were careful to take only what we felt we could use creatively, reserving the rest for forest animals and time. Opportunities for sand and water play were met with unbridled, childish joy as we borrowed directly from nature (rather than buying from Wal-Mart). We frequently took turns photographing the fruits of our exploits and our smiling, grimy faces for posterity.

The following list of supplies will infuse a child's homeschooling experience with imagination. The list is not intended to be exclusive but to serve as a basis for establishing your own version of a homeschooling "classroom".

List of Supplies—Up To Age Five

- Assorted household items, such as cotton swabs, sparkles, glues, feathers, magnets, buttons, yarn, beads, old toothbrushes, erasers, paperclips, felt, elastic bands, straws, tape, Popsicle sticks, fabric scraps, sequins, dried pasta, rice, beans, lace, ribbons, etc.
- Baskets for gathering and holding treasures
- Beeswax for manipulating and creating
- Blocks of various sizes and shapes
- Boxes of a variety of sizes
- Cardboard of different textures and weight
- Clay that can be baked for permanence
- Coloured sidewalk chalk
- Doll house
- Dolls, puppets and stuffed animals

- Dress-up clothes and old jewellery
- Easel for spontaneous art projects
- Lego
- Natural objects such as seashells, stones, nuts, pine cones, sand, etc.
- Painting supplies—water colours, poster paints, tempera paints, good quality brushes, old shirts to use as smocks, rags for clean-up, newspapers to cover floor, etc.
- Plastic animals for abstract play
- Play dough for manipulating and creating
- Poster board
- Supplies for sand and water play, such as buckets, spoons, measuring cups, etc.
- Scrapbooks for projects
- Silk scarves to serve as wings, tents, accessories, clothing, etc.
- Sponges of various sizes and shapes
- Toy cars, trucks, etc.
- Tricycle, bicycle, wagon, etc.
- Various musical instruments such as maracas, recorders, drums, etc.
- Equipment for a variety of sports, including all types of balls, skipping rope, protective pads and/or helmets for cycling, etc.
- An assortment of types, colours, quality and textures of paper
- Wax crayons, preferably of the best quality (I opted to reject water-soluble felt pens since texture and depth were harder to accomplish with these devices).

We also revelled in the delights of our daily singing and storytelling routines, often performing these activities in conjunction with our out-door adventures. These activities were voluntary in nature (pun intended!) and transpired with spontaneity and utmost silliness. For inspiration, children's music tapes and compact disks were chosen with care and due diligence.

What follows is a list of nursery rhymes, songs and finger plays that were dearly loved by my children throughout their early years.

List of Nursery Rhymes, Songs and Finger Plays—Up to Age Five

- All Around the Mulberry Bush

- The Ants Go Marching
- Baa, Baa, Black Sheep
- Boys and Girls
- Cackle, Cackle, Mother Goose
- Dance to Your Daddy
- Davy, Davy Dumpling
- Dickery, Dickery Dare
- Diddle, Diddle, Dumpling
- Down at the Station
- A Diller, A Dollar
- Eeny Meeny Miny Moe
- Elsie Marley's Grown So Fine
- Eencey Weencey Spider
- The Farmer in the Dell
- Father and Mother and Uncle John
- Grandma's Spectacles
- Handy Spandy
- Head and Shoulders
- Here We Go 'Round the Mulberry Bush
- Hey Diddle Diddle
- Hickory Dickory Dock
- Hokey Pokey
- Hot Cross Buns
- The House That Jack Built
- Horsie, Horsie
- How Many Miles to Babylon?
- Humpty Dumpty
- Hush A Bye Baby
- Hush Little Baby
- I Had a Little Nut Tree
- I Saw a Ship A-Sailing
- I See the Moon
- Ice Cream
- It's Raining, It's Pouring
- I've Been Working on the Railroad
- Jack and Jill
- Jack Be Nimble
- Jack Sprat
- Kookaburra
- Ladybug! Ladybug!
- Little Bo Peep

- Little Boy Blue
- Little Bunny Foo Foo
- Little Jack Horner
- Little Miss Muffet
- Little Robin Redbreast
- London Bridge is Falling Down
- The Man in the Moon
- Mary Had a Little Lamb
- Mary, Mary, Quite Contrary
- Michael, Row Your Boat Ashore
- Monday's Child
- My Bonnie Lies Over the Ocean
- Oats, Peas, Beans and Barley Grow
- Oh, Where, Oh, Where has My Little Dog Gone?
- Old King Cole
- Old Mother Hubbard
- One for the Money
- One, Two, Buckle My Shoe
- Over the River
- Pat-A-Cake, Pat-A-Cake
- Pease Porridge Hot
- Peter, Peter, Pumpkin Eater
- Peter Piper
- Polly, Put the Kettle On
- POP! Goes the Weasel
- Pussycat
- The Queen of Hearts
- Rain on the Green Grass
- Ride a Cock Horse
- Ring Around the Roses
- Row, Row, Row Your Boat
- Rub-A-Dub-Dub
- See, Saw, Marjorie Daw
- She'll Be Comin' Round the Mountain
- Simple Simon
- Shoo Fly
- Sing a Song of Sixpence
- Skip to My Lou
- Smiling Girls, Rosy Boys
- Solomon Grundy
- Star Light, Star Bright

- Teddy Bear, Teddy Bear
- There Was a Crooked Man
- There Was an Old Woman Who Lived in a Shoe
- This Little Piggy
- This Old Man
- Three Blind Mice
- Three Little Kittens
- To Market, To Market
- Tom, Tom, the Piper's Son
- Trot, Trot, to Boston
- Twinkle, Twinkle, Little Star
- Vintery, Mintery
- Warm Hands, Warm
- Wash the Dishes
- Wee Willie Winkie
- What are Little Boys Made of?
- What are Little Girls Made of?
- Where is Thumbkin?
- Yankee Doodle.

Story-time ensued without any preconceived strategy or schedule. It was always presented (and received) with genuine enthusiasm and commitment. Books were chosen for their artistic merit, spirit and significance. They were read aloud with dedication to the knowledge that diversity, matched with beauty and love of the written word would encourage and nurture future readers. We discovered that beautifully crafted words and the images they presented could often be more magical than a book's illustrations. Our appreciation of words nourished our collective love of reading together, and we always greatly anticipated our weekly visits to the local library, a treasure trove with its seemingly unlimited supply of wonderful books.

The following represents a number of authors whose work I especially respected and the children particularly enjoyed. The list is not meant to be exclusive but simply to serve as a potential source for stocking your own homeschooling library. It may also be necessary in some cases to compare various publications of the authors work in order to decide on an appropriate edition.

List of Authors—Up To Age Five

- Barbara Helen Berger
- Beatrix Potter
- Cicely Mary Barker
- Elsa Beskow
- James Herriot
- Ludwig Bemelman
- Robert McCloskey
- Thornton Burgess
- Tomie De Paola

I did not actively venture to teach my children to read at this time or any other. Unlike many educational mandates for this age group, I felt that this introduction, especially at such a young age, might be dangerously premature since, aside from the occasional question about a particular letter or symbol, neither child exhibited any interest in reading. By imposing my own selfish agenda on my children, I sensed that I would be detracting from their delight in books and undermining their delicate self-confidence. Occasionally I would draw their attention to the words as I read them, but ultimately, I considered it most important to follow their lead. I wanted to infuse a genuine love of books and reading in my children and not have the pleasurable act of reading develop any negative connotations for them. The children regularly witnessed my own enjoyment of reading and I believe that this gave them a more meaningful understanding than my dogmatically teaching them to read would have. I knew instinctively that they would learn to read when they were ready and on their own terms.

POTENTIALLY NEGATIVE SOCIALIZATION was perhaps our principal motivation for keeping our children out of a school. We knew that with homeschooling we could avoid many of the possibly harmful interactions present in a school environment. My experience has been that homeschooling parents take their intrinsic duties very seriously and that they exhibit an almost instinctive recognition of the importance of community in raising children. By establishing connections with the local homeschooling support group, relationships can be promoted with other families who share similar ideologies and sensibilities. Arranging occasional social events often proves to be an uncomplicated way to get together with like-minded families.

I was fortunate enough to reside in a community where a home-schooling support group, though relatively new, had already been established. Many families in my community deem homeschooling a life-style choice that begins the instant their children are born, so locating other homeschooling families with very young children was surprisingly effortless. My initial foray into this group began at the regional library, locating that very first contact number.

But for many who are new to homeschooling, this may not be such a straightforward enterprise. It may even be necessary to take the initiative and establish yourself as the primary contact for other home-schooling families. This can be achieved by providing your name and phone number to the local library, district recreational centres and area phonebooks. It is also useful to explore the Internet for neighbouring ho-meschooling groups. Establishing connections wherever possible only serves to strengthen the community. I believe that it is fundamental to homeschooling to ensure that children benefit from every possible advantage and this sometimes calls for effort on the part of a parent to convert fantasy to reality. By making every attempt to create a meaningful environment in a convivial community, your children not only benefit, but so does the village at large.

Similarly, the organizing of field trips to local historical sites, natural wonders, landmarks, businesses, science centres, museums, etc. may require your initiative. Exposing a child to diverse and engaging experiences has the potential to ignite curiosity and learning to an extent unmatched by the simple exploration of books.

If your children exhibit marked interest in a particular subject matter, or if exposure to a specific phenomenon is clearly beneficial, it is entirely likely that there will be others in your homeschooling community who would be interested in participating in this activity as well. By making contact with other homeschooling families and welcoming their inclusion in these activities, a real sense of community is reinforced.

AS NORTH AMERICANS witness escalating obesity in children, a failure to maintain adequate nutrition is only one of the issues being closely examined. Coupled with poor eating habits, the consequences of excessive television viewing and computer use—lack of exercise and lethargy—are also being implicated. Because of these compelling health issues, and also the potentially submissive nature of each medium, our family adopted measures to severely limit their influence.

Television viewing was limited to roughly an hour and a half every two weeks or so, and computer usage was restricted to one hour per week. Television programs were closely scrutinized, computer software was carefully chosen to ensure appropriate content, and Internet use was faithfully monitored. As parents, we embraced our status as role models for our children, so we also limited our own personal indulgences in these media as much as possible.

Self-education is perhaps the most rapid channel to meaningful knowledge. I found this to be particular true when the children first began to show an interest in using computer software. Once we'd installed suitable software and given the children enough instruction that they would avoid frustration, I would routinely let the children have complete control over their actions on the computer. I didn't spend my time hovering or coaching as I had confidence that they would triumph unassisted. It may have appeared at the outset that they were simply amusing themselves, wasting time manipulating the computer software, but this playful recreation was vital to their taking ownership of the medium. Invariably, as they progressed in measured steps, they acquired a keen sense of their capabilities and the software's intended merits, and gained the confidence necessary to make meaningful connections. However, since most of the children's day was devoted to self-directed preoccupations that employed tangible objects, over time, television and computer use became less attractive to them. The inherently passive nature of these pursuits was not conducive to maintaining the children's customary activity levels and actually seemed to strain their bodies and minds.

While athletics are an essential pursuit for every child regardless of age, I believe athletic programs must be chosen with the utmost care. Often, to the absolute detriment of young children, the pleasure of sport is removed in favour of unyielding rules and steadfast procedures. Effort should be made to engage a child in physical activity for the sheer joy that movement offers, not simply for the attainment of new skills. There is little reason to pursue an organized athletic program if a child's overall benefit and enjoyment are being diminished due to inappropriate methods or a generally negative environment. If a suitable program is unavailable, it may become necessary for a parent to establish a fitting alternative. Consulting your homeschooling community is often beneficial given the likelihood that other members may have similar requirements or may be able to offer valuable information about locating resources.

While self-directed, uninhibited free-time is crucial for the physical, spiritual and mental development of young children, elements of a daily routine also benefit children substantially. The habitual rhythm of a day enhances a child's ability to remain focused, offers a feeling of security and contributes to a child's growing self-confidence. Being able to faithfully identify and predict the routine events of each day bolsters a child's feeling of control, reduces stress and smoothes transitions. By embracing a daily predictable structure and accepting the ebb and flow of each day, a child's natural, unfolding rhythm is nurtured.

Abiding by a routine has potential health benefits as well. Establishing a consistent practice of brushing teeth at least twice per day, washing up at mealtimes, bathing regularly and getting adequate sleep all serve to nurture the well-being of a family. Furthermore, by launching nutrition as a habit, consuming processed food, additives, artificial colours and refined sugars are curtailed promoting optimum health, connections to the land, knowledge of where foods come from and a lifelong habit of health.

WHILE WE TRIED to be consistent in our daily lives, flexibility and spontaneity remained our guiding companions. Possibility was invited at every turn and embraced as a supplement to our natural vitality. We saw potential present in everything. Because life is dynamic and ever-changing, I feel children need to fully embrace flexibility to genuinely comprehend their world. Ongoing life lessons in adaptability provide the children with the experience to deal more effectively with change. As a homeschooling parent too, it is essential to be adaptable and receptive to your constantly evolving environment just as your children must work to achieve a level of comfort in adjustment on their journey through childhood.

WHAT FOLLOWS IS a description of two particularly representative days in our early homeschooling passage. My hope is that this practical, day in the life narrative will further clarify the issues presented in the preceding discussion. The children were ages four and five at the time.

Captain's Logbook—Up To Age Five

My husband and I are abruptly awakened at close to seven o'clock on **Monday** morning by the muffled thuds of two chasing sets of feet welcoming a new day. I hastily enter the washroom, squinting through half open eyes, struggling to pull myself into some semblance of consciousness. I perceive a resounding crash as two little rascals, thus far unseen but observable in my mind's eye, prepare their own breakfasts. I choose to markedly abbreviate my morning routine and veritably gallop to the kitchen in time to witness two diminutive rogues lined up at the counter in a nest of corn flakes. I step into the kitchen, mindful of the sound and unpleasant sensation of cereal being crushed under my slippers, and reach for my already brewed coffee. Setting the table, I motion for the children to progress to their chairs. Cereal prepared (and swept up!), juice poured and noise abating, my husband enters to muted good mornings and to our family's common place, comfortable, controlled chaos.

After an optimistically, nutritious breakfast of cereal and milk, a colossal helping of humour, and "Good-bye!" wishes to Daddy, the children race to their respective rooms to choose play clothes for a routine day of childishness, discovery and family. I hurriedly clear up the breakfast dishes, make my way to the shower and consult my internal calendar for counsel on the upcoming day.

After my shower, I guardedly enter my son's bedroom and my assistance is promptly requested. As I lasso his befuddled focus, my daughter proposes to brush her teeth and hair, wash her face and "make her bed". My son's transformation complete, I enter my daughter's room to offer aid. Perfect in their jumbled disarray, the children merrily engage in uninterrupted free-time, blocks towers and blanket covered chairs providing an hour of creative play and uninhibited fun.

As interest in their own activities wanes and grumblings can be discerned from the playroom, I stride in to suggest we partake in some singing. I have found that in order to avoid many behavioural issues (and sometimes outright combat!), it is important to watch for tell tale signs of disharmony. By suggesting outgoing, gregarious time after a period of concentrated focus (and vice versa), many conflicts and negative behaviours can be happily circumvented. Following this ebb and flow on a daily basis lends itself well to more meaningful experiences as well.

We gather in a circle, performing finger plays and actions songs with silliness until hunger pains break through the revelry. The children advocate for a snack of yogurt, fruit and a mass of assorted nuts, which we happily prepare with fun.

After satisfying our cravings, we proceed to the couch for a well-loved story. Beatrix Potter has proven to be a favoured author and the addition of her books to our home library has been much welcomed. The edition that we own presents the simple stories with stunning pictures and served to transport us to English gardens and rural contentment.

As our selected story draws to a close, the children are disposed to more creative play, pulling out various baskets filled to the brim with interesting objects of various shapes, colours and uses. They decide to craft pictures employing Popsicle sticks, construction paper and sand pausing very infrequently to request my assistance. Time speeds past and before our globules of paste have had time to dry, we are collectively preparing pancakes for lunch.

This afternoon, the children have their weekly skating lesson at the local recreational centre. This is a program that I have helped organize for my children and for many of the other homeschooled children in our immediate area. It is facilitated by a man whose children are also homeschooled.

We arrive just in time and as parents are encouraged to participate in the lesson, I lace up my skates as the children make their comical, clumsy journey to the ice surface. My task completed and my nerve fortified, I advance to the ice, my oldest child whirling past me as I nearly collide into one of the other mothers. Seizing my son's hand for balance, we attempt to follow the playful directions of the instructor and play side splitting games (literally!) together with the group.

As our lesson concludes, we take our leave of the merciless ice, remove our skates and choose to continue to the local library for some quiet perusal of books, relaxation and softer landings. There, we are pleased to discover the presence of good friends and are invited for a visit to their home.

Checking out our mass of books, we travel to our destination, the children talking spiritedly, eager to engage in rampant free-time, while I recall the merits of my friend's nice pliable couch. After an hour of chit-chat, we return home for some quiet time and a quick snack.

While the children devour their fruit compotes, I tussle with the mountain of ironing and clear the dishes. We have been taxed by this afternoon's events so I suggest another round of story-time to reconnect and fully unwind. We cuddle on the couch, feet up, warm and cozy, enjoying our lot.

Before long, it is time to commence supper preparations and the children elect to play in their own respective rooms. Daddy arrives home as the table is being readied and I hear exuberant voices exclaiming in the retelling of the seemingly hilarious day.

Subsequent to a simple meal, the children help load the dishwasher and make ready for their bedtime routine. A riotous bath time followed by the brushing of teeth and an abridged clean up of toys, the children are keen for a final story and goodnight kisses. It has been a hectic day and the children tumble to dreamland with nary a word of protest.

All quiet and my husband and I spend the evening discussing our respective days, pursuing our various individual pursuits (writing and book-keeping for me and guitar playing for him) and retire to bed a full hour earlier than usual. Apparently we all could use a good night sleep.

Tuesday pierces my slumber with a shriek, the sound of a distant plummet and dramatic laments. Without delay, I follow the sound of the raucous and witness my son, seated on the floor, his tear-stained face twisted in a frightful bawl, and his sister, wailing but still managing to play with a much-coveted toy dump truck. I dart to my son first and attempt to sooth his heartache with empathy and gently encourage the retelling of the foregoing events. Each child, too distressed, too aggrieved and too loudly wailing to possibly provide a coherent version of circumstances, causes me to pause, listen and consider my next move.

Apparently, silent hugs were all that were required for before long we are making our way to breakfast only to find that our dog had thrown up on the kitchen floor during the night. I sit the children down at the kitchen table, bellow loudly for my husband and proceed to do what my mother did before me and her mother did before her. I clean up after the family dog.

Breakfast late, shower late and late to my daughter's riding lesson, I clench the steering wheel hard. I am frustrated, irritable, and quickly losing my calm veneer with every harsh demand I hear myself utter. The children, sitting innocently in the back seat, begin to cry in sheer dismay, rapidly escorting me back to reality and I am instantly remorseful.

I stop the car and undo my seatbelt to better gaze at the sorrowful faces of my children. I feel wretched and I let them know how much I love them and that parents make mistakes sometimes, too. I explain to the children what I am feeling and apologize for letting my emotions run away with me. I go on to explain that everyone has emotions and it is okay to show them but it is not okay to hurt others feelings in the process.

I should have tried to remain positive and flexible in the face of mounting irritations but sometimes the frustrations catch a person off guard and unfortunate behaviour ensues. I am human but conscious of my influence on my children. The best conduct that I can put forth is to try my utmost to be the finest role model possible and be honest with my children even when I have to admit my transgressions.

As tears are dried, we all feel better and we continue our journey.

Back at home we are further calmed by Beatrix Potter and *Peter Rabbit*. After this, I invite the children to choose their next activity. My son suggests a puppet show based on the tale *Goldilocks and the Three Bears* and we spend much of the afternoon making silly, haphazard puppets out of whatever we determine remotely suitable.

After a novel interpretation of the story, we feel a bit disjointed so we set out for a hike in the woods with our infamous, shaggy dog for company. We observe the darkness of the forest, a range of water fowl, mud and even a dead bat. It begins to rain but our exploratory fortitude is not dampened. Singing *Hickory Dickory Dock* with delight we are oblivious to our soggy clothes and the many overflowing puddles.

After a while, with our baskets full of sodden treasures, we are guided home by our grumbling tummies. Tingling with high spirits, we enjoy a wholesome snack and story followed by blissful free-time. Daddy arrives home as supper nears completion, happy that we were able to triumph over the morning's adversity! The children's bedtime routine is accomplished and I relish in an evening spent alternating between writing, bookkeeping and stillness.

DURING THE COURSE of this well practiced yet flexible routine, my core beliefs have emerged and been refined. Throughout these very early homeschooling years, I have discovered that regardless of methodology or venerable goals, the most worthwhile and readily embraced course of action is found in listening with concentrated focus to a child's voiced and unspoken wishes. Ensuring that a child's needs are being met is paramount to promoting a childhood that is suitably enriched. Children, boasting a home life which supports their natural unfolding personality, flourish and gain the confidence necessary to tackle unknowns with buoyancy. With generous and unconditional love, enhanced learning with real life experience and plenty of unstructured play, fun and spontaneity, a childhood is ensured that speaks to their expanding dreams. I have endeavoured to facilitate their earliest discoveries with gentle encouragement, maximum accommodation and utmost tolerance. I strove to provide them with my time, affection and patience with the absolute certainty that the best thing that I could give them was exactly what they needed—me.

CHAPTER FIVE—AGES FIVE AND SIX

Nautical Compass—Ages Five and Six

As children reach the ages of five and six, a homeschooling parent's thoughts may turn slightly away from encouraging unstructured playtime and more to facilitating academic pursuits. However, children in this age group remain steadfastly attached to their need for movement and self-determination, genuinely driven to follow their own pursuits. They remain in the will realm.

An environment conducive to self-directed learning will allow a child's natural curiosity to flourish. As fine motor skills improve and children become physically stronger, it becomes all the more important for children to be assured that their individual needs are respected. When allowed to explore the full range of their imagination and ability, children experience the joy of making individual discoveries. When such pursuits are supported and embraced, children feel safe to test the range of possibilities. By doing so, they are best able to make sense of their world. For young children with ample choice and free-time to chart their own path and pursue self-directed whims, creative endeavours blossom as part of an enriched childhood. Children appreciate knowing that their ongoing quest for self-determination is supported. Along with such understanding comes the knowledge that if it becomes necessary, they may retreat to a parent for reassuring security and acceptance. Such true appreciation of a child's resolve and will fosters self-esteem and awareness of capability, qualities that enable true learning.

It remains greatly beneficial for a young child's day to unfold in as routine a fashion as is reasonably possible. Observing a routine lends structure to their lives and cultivates a genuine sense of security, comfort and self-confidence.

Strict or rigid deference to a schedule however, I vehemently discourage as this only serves to foster resentment and depleted self-worth in children so young. Allowing spontaneity and merriment into the day's routine day lend a warm and welcoming touch thereby creating more meaningful encounters that will be absorbed more fully.

WHEN MY CHILDREN were five and six, I created a chart to help maintain my focus and direction during the course of our homeschooling year. I referred to it primarily in times of imbalance, when the children exhibited signs of apathy or disconnection from their imaginative spirit. We used it over a nine-month period (i.e. 36 weeks), recording compliance with a check mark and regularly made efforts to maintain a certain level of flexibility while moving gently toward our objectives. Serving merely as a guide, its objectives were completed gradually—always respecting the children's natural rhythms with deference for each of their quests for selfhood. The concepts articulated on it were based on research from various websites, discussions with other homeschooling families, and inspiration from my own children.

WNC: 5-6 — Weekly Nautical Chart: Ages Five and Six

Week	1	2	3	4	5	6	7	8	9	10	11	12	13	14	15	16	17	18	19	20	21	22	23	24	25	26	27	28	29	30	31	32	33	34	35	36
Athletic Programs																																				
Baking																																				
Computer Time																																				
Crafts																																				
Craft Book																																				
Freestyle Painting																																				
Games																																				
Gardening/Yard Work																																				
Household Chores																																				
Mathematics Profile																																				
Music Appreciation																																				
Nature Hike																																				
Outside Time																																				
Science Profile																																				
Sculpting																																				
Singing and Poetry																																				
Story-time																																				
Story-time																																				
Story-time																																				
Wellness Profile																																				
	A	B	C	D	E	F	G	H	I	J	K	L	M	N	O	P	Q	R	S	T	U	V	W	X	Y	Z	r	r	r	r	r	r	Y	Z	r	r
	e			r		e			r			e			r			e			r			e			r			e			r			e
	v			v		v			v			v			v			v			v			v			v			v			v			v
	i			i		i			i			i			i			i			i			i			i			i			i			i
	e			e		e			e			e			e			e			e			e			e			e			e			e
	w			w		w			w			w			w			w			w			w			w			w			w			w

Conventional academic studies should be presented in a spirit of gentle collaboration, mindful that children this age remain in the will realm. Exacting bookwork and enforced attentiveness not only fail to establish meaningful connections for a child of this age, but serve to effectively strangle a child's will and burgeoning self-awareness. Unwanted instruction is often met with behaviours of rebellion and withdrawal because children this age perceive that although what they accomplish may be different from another's expectations, their efforts are just as acceptable and valid. By setting aside unreasonable expectations, a parent can celebrate imagination, creativity, invention and fun while tenderly promoting academics.

This has been stated earlier but it bears repeating: up until around the age of seven, children reside in a wonderfully spirited plane ruled by their will, eagerly seeking connection, growth and discovery with their hands and their daydreams. A child's natural eagerness to advance their innate imagination, to participate wholly with physical action and to imitate that which they are exposed to are the surest means to promoting academic connection. By embracing these instinctive tendencies and maintaining an environment of sincerity, acceptance and naturalism, a child's unlimited potential is unleashed.

LANGUAGE ARTS IS perhaps the most seamless academic pursuit in homeschooling. The inherent spontaneous rhythms of an average homeschooling day promote numerous opportunities to indulge in a cherished story. As in my selection of books for other ages, my collection of story titles was based on artistic merit, suitable subject matter and beauty of presentation. Because I recognized the power and simple brilliance of the printed word, I knew it could stir the children's innate intelligence and transport their spirits. I hoped to champion a love of reading by selecting books with depth and charm capable of igniting the spark of their imagination. Stimulating their imagination through story served to enrich the children's understanding of themselves and the world around them.

Although there were many authors included in our growing home library, those recognized and savoured in previous years remained vital contributors. Please refer to the preceding section for our list of much enjoyed authors.

Fairy tales and other legendary narratives were natural additions to our library. But because they are available in countless versions, I had to be vigilant in selecting appropriate tellings. I wanted to ensure that the story was delivered in a gentle fashion but still remained true to its original message. The necessity of choosing stories with age-appropriate themes was also important.

The following list of fairy tales and other classic stories complemented our homeschooling passage during this year. This list is not intended to exclude other titles but to provide a basis for selecting tales for your own homeschooling library.

Fairy Tales and Other Classic Stories—Ages Five and Six

- Beauty and the Beast
- Cinderella
- Goldilocks and the Three Bears
- Hansel and Gretel
- Henny Penny
- Jack and the Beanstalk
- Little Red Riding Hood
- Puss in Boots
- Rumpelstiltskin
- Snow White
- The Gingerbread Man
- The Little Red Hen
- The Pied Piper of Hamelin
- The Sleeping Beauty
- The Steadfast Tin Soldier
- The Three Billy Goats Gruff
- The Three Little Pigs
- The Tortoise and the Hare
- The Ugly Duckling

On chart WNC: 5-6, story-time is listed only three times per week. However, in reality, this pastime often took place many times throughout a normal day and would always occur on a daily basis over the course of a week. I chose to list it only three times per week on the chart to allow for those occasions when family obligations or other challenges offered obstacles to our plans.

To further enrich our story-time practice, a dusting of poetry was included. This addition helped familiarize the children with the musical rhythms of speech. Memorization of favourite poems and collaborative recitation served to improve the children's enunciation and nurtured a greater appreciation for the spoken word. This activity was alternated with singing practice and both were met with much enthusiasm.

Singing sprinkled our days with fun and laughter, and often a feeling of deeply rooted tranquility. While many songs and finger plays from previous years remained popular (see earlier section for a detailed list), to ensure that this activity remained fresh and truly satisfying it became necessary to acquire a larger assortment of children's music tapes/compact disks and music books. The following list of favourite songs enriched our repertoire during these years.

Supplementary List of Songs—Ages Five and Six

- B-I-N-G-O
- Do Your Ears Hang Low?
- If You're Happy and You Know It
- I'm a Little Teapot
- John Jacob Jingleheimer Schmidt
- Lindy Loo
- Lullaby
- Oh, Susanna
- Old MacDonald
- Shenandoah
- The More We Get Together
- The Muffin Man
- Polly Wolly Doodle
- Wheels on the Bus
- Where Oh Where Has My Little Dog Gone?
- You Are My Sunshine

Music appreciation was an indispensable component of our family life and contributed greatly to our joy and fulfillment in homeschooling. Freestyle guitar playing offered the children an outlet for creative expression and enjoyment. Performances often took place spontaneously and these were always welcomed eagerly. I resolutely avoided rigorous musical instruction, postponing any semblance of this regimen to a time when the children might be better able to absorb these concepts. Instead, I chose to promote the love of music with encouragement for improvisation. I wanted the children to experience the joyfulness of music without becoming preoccupied by structure, method and tone. Since my guitar playing is adequate, I acted as a kind of Pied Piper, enticing my children to accompany me for the sheer pleasure of making music together.

As stated earlier, I did not stringently attempt to teach my children to read. Instead, I did my best to establish an awareness of the printed word and gently facilitated the children's desire to read by harnessing their inherent tendencies to fantasize, move and imitate. With the abundance of literature the children experienced at home and at the regional library, they instinctively gained a sense of the connection between the symbols on the page and the communication of ideas. Occasionally, I would move my finger along the written words as I read, exposing the children to the simple mechanics of reading. As the children matured and developed more concentrated focus, they would periodically ask what the symbols represented. I would answer their questions very simply, being careful not to impose demanding concepts until they exhibited signs that they were ready to absorb a more academic response.

Once the children began to demonstrate a readiness, I began by introducing of a new capital letter each week and suggesting stories with key elements that began with that letter. We created whimsical drawings which not only supported their progress but also added a sense of fun to the process. In one of their drawings, the letter P was transformed into a precocious pig in a pink pinafore. As the children developed the drawing, he ended up playing a piccolo that was purple! In addition to this, we would reproduce giant coloured chalk letters on the pavement outside our home that the children and I would walk/run/hop/skip upon, retracing their shapes, brainstorming "rhymes" pertaining to the letter of the week. I sought to establish a welcoming introduction to the world of conventional academics—one that encouraged the children's full-fledged participation, ripe with laughter and free of pressure.

IN ADDITION TO establishing the chart, I created profiles for Mathematics, Wellness and Science—fields of study that were introduced smoothly, peppering our homeschooling year organically and instinctively. Timing for presenting various concepts and suggestions depended on my ability to remain aware of the children's interests, dispositions and natural rhythms. By presenting new ideas with respect for the children's love of fantasy, applied application and imitation, I was able to provide the children with rewarding learning experiences.

The profiles I created for my own children's learning grew from a consideration of their interests and aptitudes. This resulted in an educational arrangement customized to each of them. Because every child is unique, it is important that parents wishing to homeschool create their own learner profiles. I hope that the following profiles might serve as a framework for others.

Mathematics Profile—Ages Five and Six

- Work on a variety of puzzles together.
- Spend time presenting the qualities of the following numbers:
    - One. Cite the sun and other individual entities as examples.
    - Two. Use opposites, Mom and Dad, eyes, left and right, etc. to illustrate its features.
    - Three. Cite the primary colours, red, yellow and blue, using triangle-shaped items as reinforcement.
    - Four. Cite the seasons and a square as examples.
    - Five. As an example, note an individual's four limbs and head, their fingers and thumb, a sea star, etc.
    - Six. Cite a six-pointed star made out of two triangles as one of many examples (thereby reinforcing the concept of three).
    - Seven. Cite a square and a triangle together to make a house as an example.
    - Eight. Cite a stop sign.
    - Nine. Cite three triangles made into an evergreen tree as an example.
    - Ten. Cite fingers and toes.
- Observe the following concepts:
    - Opposites.
    - Left and right.
    - 'More than' and 'less than' using tangible objects.
    - 'First', 'middle' and 'last' using tangible objects.
- Observe and draw squares, triangles and circles.

Similar to the Language Arts ideas developed earlier, mathematical concepts were presented with an appreciation for the children's natural eagerness to fully participate. Efforts were routinely made to uphold a lifestyle which embraced discovery with hands on experience and realism thereby enhancing the continuity between life and education. By embracing the use of tangible objects and creating games to emphasize the quality of numbers, entertainment, authenticity and application were welcomed to the process. Notions inherent in mathematics such as opposites, more than and less than, left and right distinction and recognition of various shapes were accessible within the normal pursuit of everyday helping to lend realism to abstract concepts.

Creative projects also helped promote an appreciation for letters and numbers. Shaping bread dough and building clay projects gave structure to these somewhat abstract ideas while painting depictions of letters and numbers added a more complete sense of using symbols to represent abstractions.

I limited our exploration of numbers to only the first ten, to encourage a greater absorption of number concepts. Through gentle experiments, I discovered that the children gleaned more genuine benefit from experiencing the inherent quality of numbers through manipulation of tangibles, creative projects and incorporating movement than from rote recitation of order. With the measured presentation of a new number every two weeks or so, ample time was allotted for genuine understanding.

Because I welcomed the children's natural desire for movement, we regularly shifted our attention out of doors. Armed with sidewalk chalk, we produced giant numbers (like we did for capital letters) on which we would walk, tracing their structures backwards and forwards in an attempt to establish a physical appreciation for their form. This demonstrated the harnessing of kinaesthetic learning, one of the well-established, recognized modes of learning.

Nature hikes, which included our ever-willing pooch, provided yet another means for better understanding the characteristics of letters and numbers. A treasure hunt for spontaneously occurring representations of these forms—an 'A' in the crook of a branch, an '8' in a pattern of seaweed on the beach—gently enhanced their growing insight.

We found many ways to reinforce the qualities of the letters and numbers we'd learned about. Creating vibrant collages and crayon drawings, forming numbers and letters with clay and later, playing blindfold games with these creations—such creative 'play' reinforced and refreshed the children's comprehension.

THE HABIT OF routine may also be used to ensure acceptable levels of health and vitality. By striving to obtain enough rest, eat nutritious meals, and establish a habit of proper hygiene, a healthy lifestyle is established and maintained. And health benefits all aspects of life.

I created a Wellness Profile to guide us through this homeschooling year. It was intended to supplement our health routine and to provide exposure to health issues in ways that were entertaining and informative. Remember that children this age are in the will realm and learn best through hands on experience. Focusing too heavily on the academic aspects of each of these activities may encroach of a child's will and render the exercises meaningless.

Wellness Profile—Ages Five and Six

- Build an assortment of homes out of blocks, boxes or perhaps natural objects. Discuss the uses of various rooms in your home and the content of each. Note differences.
- Consider the range of clothing in a catalogue and discuss what is worn during the various seasons.
- Dance to various types of music and discuss what emotions are present with each new piece offered.
- Discuss the following:
- Food and its uses and the feeling of hunger. Put on a tea party.
- Germs and the importance of thoroughly washing hands. Also discuss the notions of visible and invisible dirt, friendly bacteria, etc.
- How blood travels through a body, clots and scabs.
- How joints work with demonstrations. It may be necessary to borrow appropriate books from the library to supplement this activity. Keep it simple and fun.
- How muscles work with a demonstration. Again, a trip to the library may be useful.
- Body heat. Contrast mammals with cold blooded animals.
- The ways skin is useful. Have the children consider how humans keep cool or warm up.
- The concepts of hot and cold using a heating pad, ice cubes, the sun, etc.

- The emergency phone number 9-1-1 and plan what to do in the event of an emergency. Put on a play to illustrate this situation and any resultant actions. Discuss how a body gets better.
- The importance of wearing helmets when riding bikes and participating in other sports.
- The proper names for genitalia with an emphasis on privacy.
- The use of seatbelts and other equipment in a car that are designed to keep us safe. Go on a mini-field trip to the car and the have children manipulate their seatbelts and locate other safety devices.
- The value of home rules and taking responsibility.
- Where babies come from and the process of being born.
- Enjoy finger painting and have children aid in the cleanup.
- Gather an assortment of pillows and discuss bedtime and the value of a good night's sleep.
- Have fun preparing a play dough or clay "meal".
- Have the children contribute to the weekly grocery list. On grocery day, have them pay particular attention to the cost of the listed items.
- Identify the body parts of an assortment of stuffed animals.
- Look at fingernails and discuss how they are used.
- Look through a medicine cabinet and pay particular attention to warning labels.
- Look through a photo album and note how the family has changed through the years. Discuss how a person changes as they age, becoming an adult and growing old.
- Make a friendship poster.
- Observe living and non-living things.
- Observe various types of toothbrushes and discuss the value of dental hygiene.
- Plan a field trip to a doctor's office. Discuss x-rays and treating injury.
- Plan a field trip to a natural history museum and pay particular attention to old bones and skeletons.
- Play "follow the leader" and discuss the value of following directions and taking turns.
- Play at washing a doll's hair and discuss the value of hair health. Look at magazines to observe different hair styles.
- Play restaurant.
- Practice bouncing a variety of balls and hold a jumping contest. Discuss the importance of exercise and physical move-

ment in our daily lives and also the value of rest. Have the children check their pulse after vigorous activity and discuss how the heart is the body's pump.

- Practice reciting your address and phone number. Add a musical element to make it easier to learn these long strings of numbers.
- Prepare a tea party and focus on using polite manners.
- Talk about what is meant when we refer to the environment and observe our own environments: our respective rooms.

SCIENCE WAS A realm of learning that was easy to track each week. Nature hikes provided ample exposure to the physical world and provided many opportunities for applied discovery. Hands-on manipulation of natural objects—whether in the forest, on the beach or in the garden—helped advance connections, enabling uninhibited curiosity to thrive. My own knowledge and sincere love of nature contributed to the children's reverence for the outdoors and encouraged their pursuit of meaningful experience in nature.

To supplement our frequent voyages into the natural world, I produced the profile provided below, with the intent of inspiring further discovery. It was intended to be done in order but as always, flexibility is paramount.

Science Profile—Ages Five and Six

- In the Fall:
- Establish a seasonal table and adjust it to commemorate each passing season.
- On a nature hike, adopt a "wonder" tree and watch how it changes throughout each season.
- Use apples as a tool for applying different senses. Cut one open, inhale its scent. Listen to the crunch when you take a bite, etc. Cut one open to discover the apple star. Make up a story as to how it got there—- perhaps this is where stars go at the end of each night.
- Discuss the term science and what it means to be a scientist.
- Use an empty plastic bottle (2 L size) that has been cut in half to establish a terrarium. Observe how the plants in it change over time.

- Take a trip to the local library and borrow books on migrating animals. Discuss animal homes.
- When you spot a rainbow, make up a story about it.
- Spend time playing in raked leaves and demonstrate the nature of camouflage. See who can hide their leg or hand best.
- Observe the beauty of spider webs.
- Take a trip to the local library and borrow books on spiders and fish.
- Make up a story as to why deciduous trees loose their leaves in the fall—perhaps the leaves are given to provide a blanket for baby dandelions.
- Observe clouds and make up a story about the "life cycle" of a cloud.
- Make fruit pies in season.
- In the Winter:
- Observe deciduous and evergreen trees taking time to feel the different textures of bark.
- Maintain a bird feeder and replenish it throughout the season.
- Pretend to be forest animals getting ready for winter.
- Observe squirrels preparing for winter.
- Shove toothpicks into a sweet potato and suspend it in a glass of water. Watch for growing roots and leaves. Observe how it changes over the season.
- Recall the previous season and paint pictures to illustrate how it contrasts with the current season.
- Place recently gathered natural objects in a bag and play a blindfold game attempting to uncover what each object is by touch alone. Discuss skin sensors.
- Make shakers using assorted items like rice, beads, beans and pebbles. Take special note of the different sounds these objects produce when shaken. Discuss the concepts of high and low sounds and how a mouth moves when it makes each of these sounds.
- Visit the local library and borrow books on deserts, arctic regions and forests.
- Make pancakes with maple syrup and discuss where the syrup comes from.
- Engage in free-time with magnets.
- Go for a walk at night, observing how it is different from a walk during the day. Use a variety of senses.

- Visit the local library and borrow books on the types of deer or other wildlife found in your region.
- Gather three dried kidney beans in a thoroughly dampened paper towel and place in a glass with the beans toward the outside for easy observation. View roots, stem and leaves over the coming weeks and months.
- Discuss five senses while baking bread.
- Play with an assortment of keys and locks.
- In the Spring:
- Observe changes that indicate the arrival of spring and contrast that season with winter.
- Purchase various seeds and plant an indoor garden to be transplanted outside as it gets warmer.
- Visit a local pond and note when migrating birds return.
- Go on a nature expedition to the backyard armed with magnifying glasses to better observe plants. Discuss the parts of a plant and their function.
- Go on a nature expedition to the backyard armed with magnifying glasses to better observe insects. Discuss the parts of an insect and their function.
- On grocery day, pay particular attention to the types of foods that are in season. Discuss the major food groups and the importance of balanced nutrition to health.
- Dig for earthworms and discuss how they benefit a garden.
- Observe dandelions, noting differences between bud, flower and seed stages.
- During a nature hike, try to spot bird's nests.
- Freeze water and melt ice cubes.
- Participate in water fun at the kitchen sink with various items and containers.
- Visit the local library and borrow books on the lifecycle of butterflies.

MANY OF THE enriching pursuits enjoyed in previous years were seamlessly maintained and enhanced for this age group. Painting continued to be a weekly activity that the children and I delighted in and wished to further develop. By encouraging the children's involvement through imitation, it was easy to introduce new methods and simple concepts. I would modestly start on my own artistic project and before long I would be joined by the children, energetically copying my straightforward techniques. By merely producing my own basic composition and championing their versions onto the page I was able to encourage experiments with primary colours, different types of paint, and even crayon and pastel drawings. This pattern of imitation led to an exceptionally creative, productive and satisfying time for all of us.

Another creative enterprise that was preserved and enhanced was participation in crafts. These activities were primarily child-directed. My role was as catalyst, littering their path with stimulating objects, motivating the children to build structures based in their imagination. We often used many of the natural objects collected during our frequent nature hikes. These always led to an interesting array of sculptures and often abstract art.

To facilitate these and other creative outbursts, it remained necessary to keep a healthy supply of quality arts and crafts materials in stock. These and others not only enhance our home "classroom", but enriched our overall homeschooling experience as well. The items listed below are really only suggested additions to the list of supplies presented in the previous section. Again, this listing is not to be considered definitive, but as a source of ideas for your own homeschooling "classroom".

Supplementary List of Supplies—Ages Five and Six

- An spirited book of craft projects (although library collections invariably contain many such books)
- Decks of cards
- Index cards
- Pastels
- Knitting needles of various sizes

During these years, athletics remained a vital component of our homeschooling experience. Nature hikes provided an effortless means to connect with nature while acquiring healthful physical exercise. Other weekly scheduled activities such as skating, swimming and gymnastics provided growing children with the self-assurance and competence necessary for development and fun. Programs were chosen not for the strict attainment of skills but to build dexterity and confidence and for the opportunity to interact with others in an active and lively environment. My participation remained a vital aspect of these pursuits and benefited me at least as much as it did my children.

Routine provided a useful way to advance maintenance of the household. Children this age can truly take on greater responsibility for the daily workings of a home. Practical familiarity with these important life skills become a routine part of each child's day. Our gentle encouragement and expectations for accountability gave each child an authentic feeling of ownership and respect for possessions. Also, because we operate a company out of our home, we gave the children rudimentary tasks that would expose them to the realities of our family business.

Despite exposure to such grown-up pursuits as a home business, the children's exposure to computer time and television watching were still greatly restricted. I limited computer time to one half hour each week and television viewing to an hour and a half every two weeks or so. I carefully monitored their choice of television programs and Internet use, and I was cautious in my purchase of "educational" software. As in earlier years, once I had determined that a particular software program was appropriate, I chose not to supervise their efforts, confident that more significant learning would occur with a more self-directed quest.

IN CONCLUSION, CHILDREN aged five or six exist in a remarkably dreamlike state, largely committed to following their own path to self-determination. Measures must be taken to ensure stimulating experience is provided with ample support for their growing strength of will. Conventional academics introduced at this time must be presented with the spirit of love and encouragement. These pursuits must be permitted to unfold in sync with a child's natural rhythm, being neither forced nor unnatural. A child needs to feel free to pursue their own propensities and inclinations, confident that their efforts will be accepted and welcomed within the routine of their day. By embracing a child's innate tendencies to imitate what they see and hear, to actively participate in activities and to apply imagination, a parent enables their offspring's meaningful encounters with the world and in effect, enhances their childhood.

BELOW IS AN account of two typical days in our homeschooling journey when the children were ages five and six. Again, my intent is simply to provide further clarification to the information provided in the previous discussion.

Captain's Logbook—Ages Five and Six

Monday arrives with brisk resolve. In an effort to take advantage of the children's growing self-reliance, I have opted to begin an exercise program for myself. Awaking at six o'clock in the hope of starting my workout by at least seven, I prepare my husband's lunch while he showers. As I finish this task, he greets me in the kitchen and grabs a steaming hot cup of coffee. It is just the two of us this morning. The children have apparently decided to catch a few more winks and we blissfully read the morning paper in silence and leisure. All too soon, my husband prepares to leave for work and the children wobble out of bed en masse. The stillness of the peaceful morning terminated, the children manage their own breakfast of cereal and milk as I prepare for my workout.

Suitably changed into tattered, ill-fitting sweatpants and t-shirt, I enter the living room ready to perspire and stretch limbs not lengthened in many years. It feels oddly familiar and acts to bolster my determination but prior to the first shadow of beaded sweat, I am joined by two little cherubs, giggling and clumsy on the floor. We stretch and complain, exclaim and exhale and twenty minutes later, I lie on the floor, exhausted and deserted by my cohorts. With much effort and a mutiny of limbs, I struggle to a standing position, stumble past the playroom to check on the children and stagger to an essential shower.

Not quite rejuvenated but certainly cleansed, I exit the washroom and encourage the children to start their morning routine. Once the children have changed into their play clothes, brushed their teeth and hair, washed their faces and made some semblance of their respective beds and I swiftly pile the dishes in the dishwasher, we elect to cuddle on the couch for a story.

This morning's selection is a simple fantasy-based fairy tale concerning dolphins, a gift from the children's grandparents. I answer their questions regarding various sea creatures in straightforward, easy to understand terms and move to the Internet for further clarification when necessary. As their interest wanes, we grab our guitars and make merry while marching through the house in tandem.

After songs are sung and instruments cry their last wail, we move to the craft table, where we consider our letter of the day: "D". We brainstorm for as many "D" words as possible and note our story about dolphins. We retrieve an assortment of vibrant construction paper and decorate "D's" with sparkles and mad colours. Glancing out our kitchen window, I observe a lovely morning so we journey outside to walk chalk "D's" forwards and backwards in the blinding sunshine.

As lunchtime approaches we return indoors to prepare a simple meal. The children campaign for quesadillas and as they gather the necessary ingredients, I take a moment to regard how capable they are becoming.

With tummies fully rounded, we make our way to the local recreational centre for the children's 1:15 gymnastic lesson. This program has been offered for many years to the local homeschooling community and is facilitated by a homeschooling mother. The children's ability has steadily improved over time and has contributed greatly to their levels of enjoyment.

With cheeks practically glowing, the lesson concludes and we proceed home for a light snack. Story-time beckons once more and we squeeze together, choosing a paperback about a gloomy dragon ("D") on a quest for his long lost fire breath. We sink into the couch.

Today happens to be the children's agreed upon computer day, so after the story they journey to my daughter's room for their weekly stint on their software. I take this opportunity to catch up on some ironing, finish off some bookkeeping details and make a few phone calls to our local homeschooling group.

I am organizing a field trip to the Natural History Museum and need to finalize numbers and appropriate times. As I lay the phone down for the last time, I announce to the children that it is time to start making supper, so they shut down and run to the kitchen. I offer them as many tasks as they can manage and before long Daddy arrives home.

Supper draws to an end with the final enthusiastic rehashing of the day's events and I advance the children to the bath tub. Afterward, with the children scrubbed, warm and ready for bed, they embrace their Daddy and head to our son's room for story-time and hugs. Another day has passed and the evening is spent catching up on a haphazard kitchen and equally haphazard household.

Tuesday unfolds as a carbon copy of Monday except that I can hardly manage to move my legs let alone lift my head! It seems my inaugural workout has already achieved remarkable results: it has vehemently dispelled any allusions I may have had that failure to maintain an exercise regiment for five years time does nothing to curb athletic prowess.

Managing to painfully struggle out of bed with the crucial aid of my husband, I practically crawl to the kitchen to grab a cup of coffee and as I do, the children race down the hall narrowly missing their vulnerable mother. Apparently, the children's previous morning's workout had little effect. With limbs complaining, I fall into my chair at the kitchen table and the children elect to prepare breakfast for me.

Bravely, I smile as I eat my jam, almond butter and honey sandwich and gingerly ask for a hug as my husband leaves for work. I continue my morning with a trip to the shower and as I lumber down the hallway, I suggest that the children begin their morning routine.

The heat of the shower sooths my aching muscles cursorily and as I emerge, I detect persistent howling and the sounds of objects being hurled against a wall. Racing into my daughter's room, I spy the source of the commotion. Apparently, one child elected for the conclusion to a game of leap frog before the other voiced concurrence and displeasure was summarily expressed—sort of. I race to separate the combatants.

I listen to both sides in this resultant war, careful to acknowledge the validity of each statement and empathize with each emotion expressed. In very basic terms, I explain that their feelings are normal and it is okay to express them but attempting to hurt another person is not acceptable. I go on to explain that it is important for them to "use their words" and if they are having trouble controlling their behaviour, they can come to me for assistance. Mindful of the importance of keeping explanations brief and uncomplicated, I advise that each child move to their respective rooms until they have cooled down.

As peaceful relations are finally restored, I again become aware of my aching muscles and tenderly make our bed and begin kitchen duty. Before long I hear the strains of children's laughter and I know that fences have been completely mended. I call out to them suggesting a story and we launch into another fairy tale, this time about a donkey.

The sun peaks through rain clouds and shines in through the front window beckoning us outdoors. With thoughts of spring, the children and I decide to plant our daffodils and tulips.

When our autumn tradition is completed, I note that what began with fresh, sparkling faces has ended with fresh, muddy faces—a job well done. We head into the forest for a much deserved break, selectively loading our baskets with treasures as we wander. These we will utilize in countless projects over the course of many upcoming weeks.

We stroll through the woods locating impressions of "D's" in various branch formations and predictably conclude our hike with a visit to our "wonder" tree. We note that it is naked and a carpet of multi-coloured leaves hides our boots. Hungry yet reluctant to exit the grandeur of the forest, we amble home to prepare a lunch.

Once lunch is concluded and have appetites abated, we decide to complete various craft projects, applying the number two in a range of incarnations. We form construction paper two's, glittering and sticky. We discuss opposites and paint the sun and the moon on black art paper with a sprinkling of salt. And finally, we add a generous helping of the letter "D" to create comical illustrations of two deer playing with two dogs while pursuing two donkeys.

As clean up commences, we discuss the importance of washing up with soap and water and various other wellness concerns. The children offer their own ideas and observations and our discussion conducts us to the maintenance of our fishbowl.

We have had "Goldie" for two years now and the children have been gradually assuming more responsibility for cleaning his bowl. With my help, they gather all the necessary supplies and conduct the preceding with splashing savoir faire.

Once "Goldie" is rescued from his weekly test of survival, I suggest we make some bread. The dough is divided among the three of us and as I elect to follow our earlier theme and shape my section of dough into two's and D's, the children follow their own schemes. They create various incarnations of indistinct, malformed yet complete, dough blobs.

We pop our creations into the oven and start supper and just as Daddy returns home from a long day, the power goes out. This is quite a normal occurrence on the west coast of Canada given the countless trees that invariably topple onto power lines on virtually any remotely windy day. We hunker down, enjoying the stillness and quiet of powerlessness but soon, the familiar clattering and buzzing of power returns. The children are disappointed that this was so short lived so after our resuscitated supper we imagine the power has gone out again and light every candle we own to light up the night.

We roast marshmallows in the fireplace and celebrate the brilliance of the full moon. Bedtime arrives and we all conspire to stay up a bit longer, enjoying the quiet evening together. Tomorrow we will be a little more tired but also a little more delighted in our lot.

CHAPTER SIX—AGES SIX AND SEVEN

Nautical Compass—Ages Six and Seven

Children aged six and seven require frequent assurance and nurturing as they continue to develop their self-esteem. They continue to crave respect and require support along their journey toward their adult identity. It is with this in mind that honouring a child's natural rhythms and establishing soothing, reliable routines remain vital to the development of a child in this age group.

Since the best kind of knowledge can go no further than your experience, safe exchanges remain vital. A parent's sincerity, consideration and love furnish a temperate, protected harbour in which children can momentarily escape the unknown and gather the resolve necessary to meet challenges directly. The ability to trust your pledge of safe exchanges is paramount at this age since children must feel absolutely secure and fortified in order to move forward. Children's mistakes should be handled with empathy to facilitate their self-determination.

As noted previously, it is of utmost importance to make a conscious effort to eliminate any unrealistic demands you may have for your children. Children are exceptionally cognizant of their limitations and mistakes and require a parent's unconditional acceptance of them without judgment. Life is an ongoing process, and it is only through trial and error that children can own their own experiences. Expectations need to be reasonable so that children may move in their world and truly learn from their encounters. Statements must be tempered with love, understanding and compassion, allowing small transgressions to fall by the wayside. It is in the spirit of kindness that confidence, profoundness and love are created.

A parent's ultimate responsibility as a home educator is found in facilitation of knowledge, not the amassing of layers. It is essential to be fully committed to aiding a child's pursuit of self-education. No individual can disclose to another concepts that are not already resting undeveloped in the genesis of their own comprehension. In other words, you cannot completely appreciate an idea unless it is fully developed and nurtured from within. A primary function of a home educator to those of this tender age is to aid only when asked. Until assistance is authentically requested, children will learn effectively and will direct their own education creating understanding. I have also observed that children should be periodically presented with new, enticing and interesting material to ensure growth and to open doors that may otherwise have remained closed. This scattering of appealing subject matter becomes a principal focus over the coming years, and must be presented honestly, trusting your children to process the information individually and at their own pace.

Perhaps the greatest enhancement to homeschooling children of this age group is the advanced employment of democratic commitments. As a homeschooling parent, you have an enormous responsibility. Providing safe assembly, eliminating unrealistic expectation and providing compassionate facilitation often come naturally and instinctually to a conscious parent. Bestowing children with complete knowledge is quite another practice entirely. I feel it is important to accept that you can only speak to others of your own wisdom but cannot supply others with this wisdom. At this age, a child is often ready to assume some form of responsibility for their own education in so much as they may commit to a certain level of academic discipline. What this involves is an awareness of a homeschooling parent's responsibilities. Children at such a young age cannot fully comprehend a parent's true responsibilities but I believe they can appreciate the importance of being exposed to what life has to offer.

Democratically gaining a commitment from your children to strive for openness to new things becomes increasingly important. Any proposal made must be wholly reasonable and all parties involved must feel genuinely comfortable. It is vital, however to remain flexible since modification of strategy is not only a common occurrence but is often an essential feature of any rewarding commitment. The goal is for a parent and child to feel as though they are equal members of the same team. A parent's role is as facilitator to their children's education and a child's role is to be fully committed to openness and active participation in their own homeschooling voyage. Focus remains child-led but the journey must be sprinkled with engaging subject matter. Not everything presented will be accepted to a child's heart but exposure to the dwelling of knowledge does help lend wings to potential. In the end, really all that you can do as a homeschooling parent is reveal the path to a child's ocean. The rest is up to them.

I FOUND IT useful to again produce a nine-month chart to help maintain focus and provide a means for inspiration. This chart was used solely as a guide enabling our family to remain motivated while at the same time embracing flexibility. It became a means for scattering appealing subject matter in the children's path—matter that could be digested or left for another day.

Weekly Nautical Chart: Ages Six and Seven

WNC: 6-7

Week	1	2	3	4	5	6	7	8	9	10	11	12	13	14	15	16	17	18	19	20	21	22	23	24	25	26	27	28	29	30	31	32	33	34	35	36
Athletic Programs																																				
Baking																																				
Calendar-Moons, B'days,																																				
Computer Time																																				
Crafts																																				
Freestyle Painting																																				
Household Chores/Gardening																																				
Mathematics Profile																																				
Music Appreciation																																				
Nature Hike																																				
Outside Time																																				
Science Profile																																				
Sculpting																																				
Singing and Poetry Practice																																				
Story-time																																				
Story-time																																				
Story-time																																				
Wellness Profile																																				
Occupation Fieldtrips																																				
Scrapbooks																																				
1st Trimester																																				
Two letters Introduced																																				
Writing/Sounding of Letters																																				
Tang.Objects-Sum up to 20																																				
2nd Trimester																																				
Word Genera/Reading Games																																				
Reading games																																				
Mathematics Games																																				
3rd Trimester																																				
Creative Writing - Silly Stories																																				
Reading Aloud Practice																																				
2 Consonant Pairings/Games																																				

As noted in earlier sections, up until around the age of seven, children learn best though their vigorous imaginations, by careful imitation, and with their active participation in all aspects of life. This age group still exists largely in the will realm but their feeling realm is slowly beginning to awaken. It is with this in mind that many of the ideas presented in the sections about earlier years are carried over into this age category with added emphasis on storytelling—how children entering the feeling realm learn best.

IN MANY OF today's institutions of traditional learning, a child of six or seven experiences intense pressure to learn to read, write and become proficient at basic mathematical skills. Such undue pressure can create debilitating stress for a child not ready for these pursuits and often turns out to inhibit learning. By merely exposing a child to novel and appealing concepts, children will incorporate these basic skills when they are ready, producing a much more fulfilling learning environment.

It is on these grounds that Language Arts is presented in a similar fashion as in the previous year but with the addition of lower case letters. Using story, two letters are introduced each week during the first trimester. These are then incorporated into various activities during that week. Recalling letter illustrations from the previous year provides children with continuity and confidence and helps to gently unfold the meaning of ideas. Spying letters in nature when engaged in hikes through the woods, sketching gigantic, chalk drawn letters for walking forward and backward, craft projects, etc. all work toward understanding through imitation and active participation.

During the second trimester of this homeschooling year, the children began to exhibit signs that they were ready for the introduction of word genera or families. These were introduced by means of gentle encouragement through reading games. In these games, process was always the focus, not winning or losing. Since a child desperately desires independent accomplishment (which in turn strengthens comprehension), it is important to respect a child's autonomy and help only when asked. As young children gain proficiency, reading practice becomes a vastly rewarding activity opening doors to a whole new magical world of discovery and achievement.

Provided below are instructions for a simple reading game. All that's needed is any board game that would ordinarily use dice to dictate player moves. By replacing the dice with construction paper cards, a new game is created—one that enhances a child's command of reading. Each week, when we played the game, I introduced three new word families, always considering the children's comfort and their familiarly with the previous week's batch.

Reading Game—Ages Six and Seven

- Create two piles of three-by-five inch construction paper cards in two different colours for the following:

  - One pile with the following consonants: t, p, d, l, r, n, w, s, m, b, j, v.

  - One pile with the following word families: on, op, ew, ib, ad, ag, aw, um, un, ay, ed, et, id, ig, ill, im, is, in, ip, ob, og, or, ore, ot, ow, ox, an, ap, ub, ug, up, ut, ar, at, eg, en, it, ix, am, ell.

- For the second pile, randomly assign a value of up to ten for each card (for example, the card with 'ew' may be assigned a value of 4, the card with 'eg' may be assigned a value of 8).
- In place of throwing dice, have a player choose one card from the first shuffled pile (consonants) and one card from the second shuffled pile (word family). The player must try to pronounce the word created and move forward the assigned number of spaces.
  - Tip: I have found that it is sometimes easier for a child to say the word family card first and then add the single consonant to the front of that card and then attempt to pronounce the created word.

Experience has shown me that the phrase "teaching a child to read" is an oxymoron. I did not teach my children to read. They taught themselves to read—when they felt sufficiently equipped and self-assured. As a result, they both love to read. My contribution lay in providing them with security in my arms, cooperation, empathy and respect—and above all, ample opportunities to read. I must stress that the fact that my children acquired this skill between the ages six and seven does not mean to imply that it will happen for every child at this age or in the same manner. It is not uncommon for children to learn to read closer to age nine or even later. Children need unconditional acceptance, safe harbour and support on their individualized journeys. They will learn to read. The timing is up to them.

Some of my children's favourite authors are listed below. All of them have written first readers that my children thoroughly enjoyed. Again, this list is meant solely to provide a potential foundation for your home library.

List of Authors—First Readers—Ages Six and Seven

- Arnold Lobel
- Cynthia Rylant
- Dr. Seuss
- Else Holmlund Minarik
- Margaret Wise Brown
- Peggy and Herman Parish
- Sam McBratney
- Stan and Jan Berenstain

A child's skill at reading does not preclude a parent's need to continue reading to their children on a daily basis. On the contrary, it becomes crucial since a child's ability to read is often an indication of expanding comprehension and your active participation helps advance aptitude. Story-time still needs to be met with the same exuberance and joy as in previous years open to a child's query and comment. It should remain a vital part of a child's day and will enhance their ongoing desire to discover meaning through the printed word.

As on the chart in the previous section, I only listed story-time three times per week, despite my full intention for daily observance of this practice. But because family demands occasionally altered our course, there were a few weeks when story-time was reduced accordingly. Three times per week was indicated since it seemed to be a reasonable minimum number.

Also, to supplement the previous chapter's list of fairy tales, here are some recommended age-appropriate tales to include during this year of homeschooling. Again, special attention must be given to ensure appropriate retellings of these classic stories.

Supplementary List of Fairy Tales and Other Classic Stories—Ages Six and Seven

- A Brer Rabbit Story
- Aladdin

- Ali Baba
- Androcles and the Lion
- Demeter and Persephone
- George Washington and the Cherry Tree
- Gulliver's Travels
- Icarus and Daedalus
- Johnny Appleseed
- King Midas
- Peter Pan
- Pinocchio
- Rapunzel
- Rikki-Tikki-Tavi
- Rip Van Winkle
- Robin Hood
- Saint George and the Dragon
- Stone Soup
- The Bell of Atri
- The Brave Little Tailor
- The Brownie of Blednock
- The Elves and the Shoemaker
- The Emperor's New Clothes
- The Fisherman and His Wife
- The Frog Prince
- The Gift
- The Golden Goose
- The Honest Woodcutter
- The Jungle Book
- The Little Dutch Boy
- The Little Mermaid
- The Musicians of Bremen
- The Nightingale
- The North Wind
- The Princess and the Pea
- The Selfish Giant
- The Twelve Dancing Princesses
- The Velveteen Rabbit
- The Wild Swans
- Thumbelina

As a child gains proficiency in reading and writing, introducing un-lined personal creative writing books can be very advantageous. For a child to truly benefit from this addition, these books need to completely owned and controlled by the child, freeing them to write whatever they desire in them. By using unlined paper, a child is free to more fully appreciate the structure of letters. In turn, this encourages their creative process. What is written need not be coherent or sensible nor have any meaning beyond the satisfaction gained from enlisting newly acquired skills and communicating—even in what might be construed as an extremely primitive way. It is the writing process that is of maximum value, not the composition itself.

By the third trimester, the children seemed ready to proceed to consonant pairings, so I revisited the Internet and supplemented what I found with my own ideas. What I created was a game that integrated movement with new reading skills. In an effort to keep the activity fresh and yet not overwhelm the children with too rapid introduction, I tried to introduce just two new pairings each week. The instructions for this game are as follows:

Consonant Pairings Game—Ages Six and Seven

- Make a set of three-by-five inch cards out of various colours of construction paper for the following consonant pairings:

    - cl, sc, scr, bl, br, dr, fl, sh, th, fr, spr, sw, gl, gr, pl, pr, sl, cm, sn, sp, tr, tw, ch, cr, sk, kr, st.

- Make four 'baseball' bases out of sturdy cardboard and set them out on the floor like a miniature baseball diamond.
- Have a player draw a card from the shuffled pile and have them suggest words that begin with the chosen consonant pairing.
- For each word (or semblance of a word!) that a player is able to supply, they may move forward one base. A home run is scored if four words are presented for one consonant pairing.

AS IN THE previous year, I created profiles for Wellness, Mathematics and Science studies. As before, the Wellness Profile is presented in random order but the Mathematics and Science Profiles were meant to be offered in order—but efforts should be made to remain flexible and relaxed, ensuring a natural flow to the day.

The following Mathematics Profile is provided for interest's sake. I recommend that these ideas be offered slowly for more complete absorption. Remember to remain flexible and be cognisant of the importance of a child's pursuit of individual interests. Exposure to new and stimulating ideas or things is important but time must also be given for a child to relish in their childhood.

Mathematics Profile—Ages Six and Seven

- Encourage the children to spend time practicing writing and counting the following sets of numbers:
  - One to ten.
  - 11 to 20.
  - 21 to 30.
  - 31 to 40.
  - 41 to 50.
  - 51 to 60.
  - 61 to 70.
  - 71 to 80.
  - 81 to 90.
  - 91 to 100.
- Use tangible objects to illustrate shortest and longest and lightest and heaviest. Always use at least three items.
- Encourage the children to produce freehand shapes (circle, triangle and square) and then use those to create a mobile or collage.
- Discuss odd and even numbers.
- Discuss ordinal numbers (first, second, etc.).
- Encourage the children to practice counting backwards from 20.
- Encourage the children to practice counting by two's, forwards and backwards.
- Encourage the children to practice counting by five's, forwards and backward.
- Encourage the children to practice counting by ten's, forwards and backwards.
- Encourage the children to write from the number one to 100.
- Discuss the concepts of old, new, buy, sell and trade. Organize a pretend flea market.
- Play store with coins (pennies, nickels, dimes). Encourage the children to sort the coins and count change to specified amounts (i.e. 35 or 50 cents).

- Review the concepts of odd, even, ordinal numbers and sequencing practice by producing four worksheets as follows:
  - For odd numbers: numbers one to 15, leaving three blanks.
  - For ordinal numbers: numbers one to ten, leaving three blanks.
  - For even numbers: numbers one to 20, leaving five blanks.
  - Offer numbers from one to 50, leaving ten blanks.
- Review the above concepts over a number of weeks, paying special attention to areas the children appear to be struggling with.

Just as with Language Arts, mathematical concepts may be introduced through the telling of stories. For instance, rather than requiring a child's rote recitation and memorization of concepts to introduce the concepts of plus, minus, times and divide it may be more instructive to incorporate a narrative that uses items familiar to your children. For example, if your children enjoy puppies, it might be useful to incorporate puppies into a story. Through some simple research on the Internet, I found an uncomplicated story to illustrate mixed operations and adapted it for my own children.

Mixed Operations Story—Ages Six and Seven

A mother dog had a litter of puppies. One puppy (Plus) was continually dragging more bones to his mother (Equal) than he could handle. Another puppy (Minus) was exceedingly distracted and kept losing his bones on the way. Yet another puppy (Times) was very fast and took many quick trips dragging several bones to her mother each time. The last puppy (Divide) loved to share his bones with his brothers and sister.

- Tip: As the children gain a basic understanding of these ideas, it may be beneficial to have them produce an illustration of the events in the story, demonstrating the various puppies' tendencies. Later, reveal the symbols for Plus, Minus, Times, Divide and Equal and have the children include these in their illustration.

Another essential method of promoting basic mathematical concepts is through the use of tangible objects. Throughout the course of a week, I supported the children's efforts to tackle various mathematical problems. We used straws, bead, fingers, and other small object all in an effort to promote their comfort and proficiency in the manipulation of numbers.

Using games may also be considered a useful method for promoting understanding of mathematical concepts. In the act of playing a game, imagination and movement are employed to facilitate basic understanding.

What follows are simple instructions for creating a mathematics game that is suitable for this age group. Its method may be applied to any board game that uses dice.

Mathematics Game—Ages Six and Seven

- Make a set of twenty three-by-five inch cards out of various colours of construction paper and inscribe them with either plus or minus symbols.
- Make a set of fifty three-by-five inch cards out of various colours of construction paper for the numbers one through ten.
- Make two piles of number cards and one pile for symbols, being sure to shuffle each pile before proceeding.
- Have a player choose one card from each pile and have them provide the answer to the equation that is produced.
- The player then moves along the board the resulting number of spaces.

PHYSICAL ACTIVITY IS as important for growing minds as it is for growing bodies. In addition to weekly athletic programs, frequent nature hikes and regular time outside, we combined movement with as many academic pursuits as possible. Young children learn best through using their bodies, so it is vital to incorporate physical activity whenever feasible. Encouraging the use of tangible objects for mathematics practice, walking giant chalk numbers on your driveway or playing entertaining games make it easy for children to better embrace learning.

Children would much rather experience life with their full participation rather than simply watching from the wings. It is with this spirit in mind that I continued to value the children's hands-on involvement in countless activities central to housekeeping. They regularly assisted my efforts at maintaining our home, and helped perform such tasks as preparing meals, baking and basic bookkeeping. I was also able to shift their focus to gardening and yard work. Not only did it lighten my load, they learned valuable life skills too.

AS IN THE previous year, science was an area of study that was easily promoted within the average week. With frequent nature hikes (that always included our fun-loving dog), visits to local beaches, regular gardening and yard work, the natural world was easily accessible and provided many possibilities for discovery.

To supplement our regular expeditions into nature, I created the following profile.

Science Profile—Ages Six and Seven

- In the Fall:
  - Establish a seasonal table and update it to celebrate the passing seasons.
  - Observe migrating birds. Visit the local library and borrow books on animals that migrate.
  - Be alert to dramatic events such as a thunder and lightning storm and make up a story about it.
  - Observe how deciduous trees lose their leaves. Encourage the children to learn the names of trees commonly found in your area.
  - Go on a nature hike and look for different kinds of seeds (pinecones, acorns, etc.).
  - Visit the local library and borrow books on a variety of animal tracks that may be found in your area. Then, during a nature hike, search for animal tracks.
  - Note direction and placement in the sky of the rising and setting sun and observe changes that occur from day to day.
  - Note wind direction and temperature changes on a daily basis. Set up a weather station to record these simple observations.
- In the Winter:
  - During a nature hike, observe signs (both plants and animals) of the approaching change of season.
  - Visit the local library and borrow books on hibernation.
  - Observe winter birds and maintain a birdfeeder.
  - Compare a human being's winter needs with those of wild animals.
  - Decorate windows with paper snowflakes of various sizes, shapes and colours.
  - Visit the local library and borrow books about the arctic.

- Visit the local library and borrow books about animals in winter and how they adapt to the changes in temperature and conditions.
- Conduct experiments to see what floats or sinks and what is heavy or light.
- Visit the local library and borrow books on erosion.
- Demonstrate the concept of friction. Set up an incline and choose a number of items to slide down it, contrasting various surfaces.

- In the Spring:
  - Grow a tomato from seed and transplant it when the weather warms up. Encourage the children to consider what a plant needs to grow (food, water, air, sunlight).
  - Buy various flower seeds and plant them outdoors when temperatures improve.
  - Observe various animals in each of the seasons. Note how their behaviours change accordingly.
  - Go for a nature hike and pay particular attention to bird calls and other sounds in nature.
  - Observe flowers. Discuss roots, stems, and leaves.
  - Visit the local library and borrow books on the life cycle of a frog. Visit a local pond and observe frogs and other pond life.
  - Plan a garden.
  - Visit the local library and borrow books about bees. Observe them.
  - Discuss how seeds get relocated and sometimes germinate.
  - Visit the local library and borrow a book on the life cycle of a seed. Make up a story about this life cycle. Perhaps invite the children to improvise their own story.

WITH RELAXED ATTENTION to our family's daily routine, our home-schooling journey progressed steadily. We did our best to maintain a healthy lifestyle by acquiring sufficient rest, instituting good hygiene practices, and ensuring proper nutrition.

Below, I have provided the Wellness Profile that I created during this homeschooling year. My goal was to reinforce our healthy lifestyle with topics the children would find both enjoyable and instructive.

Wellness Profile—Ages Six and Seven

- Make a list of the various names you have for each member of the family.
- Investigate kitchen and bathroom cleaning products. Observe warning labels and discuss the dangers of each.
- Contact an environmental group in order to volunteer or make a donation. Consider starting an initiative individually.
- Create a poster about your own family.
- Discuss the following:
  - Herbs that heal. Plan a trip to a local health food store and note herbs that are available. Visit the local library and borrow a book on various herbs.
  - Growling tummies and what is happening.
  - House rules and why they were formed.
  - The importance of ambulances and health.
  - How a brain works.
  - Matches and candle safety.
  - The value of drinking water regularly throughout each day.
  - Traffic signs and why they are valuable.
  - The importance of covering your mouth when sneezing.
- Encourage the children to assume more responsibility for laundry day.
- Make a poster of various types of homes.
- Encourage the children to mould sculptures of their own likeness out of play dough or clay.
- Encourage the children to paint what makes them feel happy.
- Use magnifying glasses to study hands and fingerprints.
- Practice yoga breathing. Discuss how a person breathe, lungs and breathing problems. Practice yoga and a variety of stretches.
- Head to the car and play car and driver, discussing various safety concerns.
- Make a list of community safety people.
- Make a list of outside chores.
- Make a list of stores that are frequently patronized.
- On grocery day, pay particular attention to the various types of bread available.
- Place a slice of bread in a clear plastic bag and observe it over the coming weeks.
- Pay particular attention to proper tooth brushing and discuss why dental health is important.

- Explore various types of art.
- Play tea party with extreme manners.
- Schedule a visit to an optometrist for the whole family. Discuss the purpose of eye lashes and lids.
- Visit a local hair salon and get a hair cut.
- While the children are participating in water play, discuss why they should not drink this water.

MUSIC IS ALSO an important element of any childhood. Weekly singing and poetry recitation is important for vocalization exercise and enunciation and provides a family with many enjoyable afternoons. What follows is a list of popular songs that provided us with many opportunities for melodic fun.

List of Songs—Ages Six and Seven

- A Tisket, A Tasket
- Alouette
- Clementine
- Coming Round the Mountain
- Frere Jacques
- Go In and Out the Window
- Good Night To You All
- He's got the Whole World in His Hands
- Home on the Range
- Kumbaya
- Merrily We Roll Along
- Mother Earth
- Music Shall Live
- O, How Lovely is the Evening
- Oh Dear, What Can the Matter Be?
- On Top Of Old Smokey
- Over The Meadows
- Rain, Rain Go Away
- Rock- a- bye Baby
- Shortnin' Bread
- Silver and Gold
- Swinging Along
- The Gift to be Simple
- Wake Up
- When I'm Grown Up

- When the Saints Go Marching In
- Winter Good-bye
- Yellow Bird

Playing a musical instrument continued to provide inspired tomfoolery in our home. I felt that at this young age, the children benefited more completely from creating their own improvised compositions rather than through formal instruction. I did not want them to feel hindered by pressure to study precise method and tone especially when I observed that through the simple manipulation of their instruments, they seemed to be developing a keen fondness for them. Whatever instrument is chosen—even kazoo—the main focus should always remain that you play music because you love it.

Of course, crafts, sculpting and weekly painting endeavours were indispensable activities continued from previous years. I did find it increasingly necessary to obtain inspiring books on these subjects—ones that emphasized fun and creative expression.

Because our home was our "classroom", it was necessary to maintain a wide assortment of inspiring, educational resources. In addition to listings provided in previous sections, I have added a few more items which augmented our learning environment.

Supplementary List of Supplies—Ages Six and Seven

- A wide variety of books on science, history, atlases, animals, etc. for self-directed studies
- An enlivening book of painting methods
- Coloured pencils

In addition to the establishment of a seasonal table, I encouraged the children to create their own calendars each month. I felt it was too soon for them to fully appreciate the passing of time on a clock but they seemed to welcome monthly observances of the full moon and upcoming birthday celebrations. I would provide them with the basic layout of a month, and the children would independently include the numbers, words and a depiction of what that month meant to them. This simple tradition functioned to promote awareness of the passage of time in a gentle, almost reverential manner.

Field trips were a monthly occurrence spotlighting an array of occupations. These excursions were routinely organized either by me or by one of the other homeschooling parents in the surrounding area. I discovered that even though the children may have already experienced these places of business on previous field trips or other visits, each time, with their growing maturity, they gained a new appreciation. Some suggestions for occupation field trips are as follows:

List of Occupation Field trips—Ages Six and Seven

- bank
- beauty salon
- dentist's office
- doctor's office
- fire hall
- grocery store
- optometrist's office
- police station
- post office

The children's awareness of geography began within our home environment. We discussed the rooms of our home (our habitat) and what would be located in each. To supplement this homeschooling year, we shifted our focus to that of our hometown. For example, on a return voyage home from various excursions, I would periodically have the children direct us to our destination. Occasionally, we would wind up slightly astray but this too was met with enthusiasm. We considered it all a quest and sometimes we would even actively pursue misadventure by purposely getting lost.

Children amass a great deal of art and other projects over the course of any given year and this is especially true for homeschooling families. I would move their creative work into scrapbooks and would encourage the children to periodically revisit their work, recalling their adventures and artistic accomplishments. During this homeschooling year, I occasionally suggested that the children decorate their scrapbook pages, creating frames for their work. I promoted the idea that they frame their drawings in running patterns of their own choosing. These little embellishments were intended to encourage the children to work with connected pattern in preparation for cursive handwriting.

Again, computer usage and television viewing were restricted due to their innate submissive nature. Educational software, television programs and movies were chosen carefully and were rated for their capacity to promote independent learning. Internet use was carefully screened.

IN CONCLUSION, I believe that when children experience a democratically-run environment filled with sensible expectations, secure encounters, and support for their growing individuality, they will feel loved, respected and supported. Authentic confidence develops from these roots and can transport a child into domains of genuine discovery coupled with a strong love for learning.

BELOW IS A description of two characteristic days in our home-schooling passage when the children were ages six and seven. Again, this representation is here to assist in the clarification of the preceding discussion.

Captain's Logbook—Ages Six and Seven

With the insistence of our alarm clock, **Monday** begins. The house is quiet. I carefully place my feet in my slippers, listening intently for any sign of movement from other areas of the house. As I round the corner to my daughter's room, I hear the flip of a page. I spy the children awake and reading quietly in her room—quite the departure from the mornings of a few years ago.

My daughter spots me and runs to be hugged and loved. My son continues reading and grumbles that he is hungry. I choose to ignore his "wrong side of the bed" mutterings and suggest that we all head to the kitchen for toast and jam. I hope to be able to coax some pleasantries from his surly demeanour.

The children set the table as I pour myself a cup of coffee and my son questions me about what our day has in store. Monday is our "stay home and do some baking" day. He is pleased and slowly deserts his funk. I am glad that I carefully chose my battle.

After my shower and the completion of our morning routine of teeth brushing, making beds, getting changed and washing faces, the children and I travel to the kitchen to load the dishwasher. Household chores have become a routine and expected occurrence. The children will regularly help me with washing dishes, loading and unloading the dishwasher, washing clothes, cleaning the house, setting the table, meal preparation and even sundry bookkeeping duties. This is not to say that they will help me every moment I venture to accomplish these chores. I think it is important for them to pursue their own interests uninterrupted most of the time but, when I feel in need of a little help, their presence is requested.

After the dishwasher is loaded, we prepare to make bread. The children have been doing this for some time now and can virtually do this on their own. However, my participation remains necessary when it comes time to kneading the dough thoroughly. The children decide to shape their names out of their portions and before long the dough is resting.

Since today is a "stay at home" day, I commence a long overdue clean up of the house. The children settle into tidying their own rooms at the sound of the vacuum. Once these chores are completed, I advance to the washroom to scrub and polish as the children grab their dust rags and "dust" their rooms as they see fit.

I have found that over the years it is most important for the children to do their chores to the best of their ability without me stepping in to "fix" their efforts. Beds are rarely made in the traditional sense and dusting tends to be a bit haphazard, but their feelings of ownership and accomplishment remain in tact.

Once we finish our weekly house clean, we return to the kitchen to reshape our dough. With this accomplished, we gladly head to the couch for a much deserved story.

Today's first story is a favourite from Ludwig Bemelman. We discuss the role of the ambulance personnel in the story and make plans for a subsequent field trip. We decide to visit the local fire hall and I suggest we invite the greater homeschool community to this outing. I make a couple phone calls and a date and time are set. Apparently, next week's "stay home and do some baking" day will have to be rescheduled.

We journey back to the couch and the children take turns reading to me from one of their favourite first readers by Arnold Lobel. Recently, both children began reading independently. Through the years I maintained a willingness to read to them, never pressured them to read and encouraged exposure to the written word at practically every turn. Over time, the children in turn felt ready to acquire this new skill and took over full responsibility for this challenge.

As lunch time approaches, I assess our bread dough and transport our "loaves" to the oven. I warm up some leftover soup from the previous day and for "dessert", we enjoy our bread creations before they even have a chance to cool.

After lunch, the children campaign for a nature hike, so we clear the dishes and travel outside to enter the forest. We stumble along our course and admire the first semblances of spring upon our "wonder" tree. We return home to construct a welcome back spring poster to celebrate.

Today happens to also be the children's agreed upon computer day, so when we finish clearing away our splattering of glue and assorted scraps of paper, the children retire to my daughter's room to choose their software. I take advantage of this occurrence to wrestle with an unruly bookshelf, sort out some bookkeeping snafus and consider the supper menu.

In the midst of my melee, my husband arrives home after "one of those days" and he suggests we go out for supper instead. Computer time is promptly concluded but met with enthusiasm when the local Italian restaurant is suggested. As my husband's countenance brightens with each fork full, I propose we go for a night-time walk after we eat.

Arriving home with bellies filled with noodles and an abundance of fresh night-time air, our beds are summoned and we all fall asleep quickly.

Tuesday morning, I consider our day as I sort through our mounting heap of dirty laundry. I am shaken out of my reverie by the children's animated voices insisting that we invite our very good friends over for afternoon tea. I remind them that they have swimming lessons scheduled this afternoon but propose we invite our friends over for a late tea nevertheless. It is unanimously agreed upon and I place the necessary phone call.

As I recommence sorting laundry, I invite the children to tackle a craft project from a craft book acquired the previous year. They rifle through the book and I move to assist each child with their projects when asked. My daughter produces a baby dragon out of cellophane and construction paper, lightly coloured and full of imagination, and my son has constructed a series of cards out of bits of coloured paper, crayons and perhaps a bucket full of dark blue paint.

Once the familiar rumbling of the washer looms over the house, I capture our latest book of poetry and we launch further reading of our choice poems. When interest wanes, my son challenges me to a game of chess.

Recently, my son has battled with acute, poor sportsmanship and owing to this, I somewhat reluctantly meet his challenge. After twenty minutes of play, I grudgingly call "checkmate" and my son responds in characteristic, undignified wrath.

I halt his unseemly progress before he has a chance to meltdown, make firm eye contact and explain that it is okay for him to be disappointed but it is not okay for him to become verbally abusive. I continue to use some well placed "I" statements, explaining how his words make me feel and eventually, my son starts to calm down. He whispers an almost inaudible apology. Since children this age have an intense desire to preserve their dignity, I accept this apology graciously and with care, suggest we begin a different game that includes his sister.

We decide on a consonant pairings game and as we each travel around a makeshift ball diamond, we dissolve in giggles over silly words that we invent such as, floop, ploop and challyoop! We play many rounds of this game when I finally realize I must get lunch started.

After our meal, the children are eager for another distraction so we advance to the couch to enjoy a good read. We choose a book by Tomie de Paola but before the first page is completed, the phone beckons. Generally, I do not answer the phone when we are engaged in an activity but I considered that it might be my husband so I hastily answered it.

It turns out to be an individual from the local recreational centre notifying me that the pool has been closed unexpectedly for maintenance and no lessons will be taking place today. I inform the children of this glitch to their plans and they are befuddled, not knowing whether to cheer or brood.

The children truly love to swim but since they have been thoroughly enjoying their morning at home, they simply do not want it to come to an end.

After completing our book selection and engaging in various self-led activities, our friends pull up and we enjoy a pleasing visit. The children play vigorously outside on our jungle gym while the adults sip their tea in homey, warm comfort.

All too soon, we are calling, "Good-bye!" as our friends leave, happy but spent. I begin contriving menu selections and the children settle down for some much needed quiet time. My husband returns home to baked potatoes, steamed vegetables and salmon salad sandwiches, warm and inviting. The evening closes with stories and lights out.

OUR PRIMARY AMBITIONS each week centre on planting firm roots in family, providing reprieve and safe harbour, facilitating experience through exposure to new and enticing subjects and offering support on our children's journey of self determinism. But perhaps the most important objective in any given week lies in providing our children with a childhood, filled with their own discoveries, accomplishments and joys.

CHAPTER SEVEN—AGES SEVEN AND EIGHT

Nautical Compass—Ages Seven and Eight

A child crossing into this age group is a child who is beginning an important stage of transition. They are becoming more autonomous, bold and courageous and may be very spirited. They are parting with their early childhood tendencies and moving further toward independence. Strong is their sense of self-sufficiency and they tend to harbour a fervent need for self-directed decision making. Children of this age group tend to strive for mounting control over their own lives and require a parent's constant acknowledgement of their desire for self-rule. I feel, however, that they still require a parent to provide safe harbour as a respite in times of strife.

A child this age is leaving behind the dream-like, will state of early childhood and entering a new realm of emotional connections (i.e. the feeling realm). Where previously they may have felt content to remain at home, they now crave social interaction with their peers. This is not to say that the parental relationship should be replaced by a child's contemporaries. A child still requires the support of a parent, but peers play a more pivotal role in their journey to individuality.

During this period, I remained dedicated to facilitating my children's pursuit of their individual interests. As they became increasing more capable and confident, my support and encouragement remained important but my role was gradually becoming that of the occasional advisor. I sought to ensure that interruptions were made only when absolutely necessary and often found that my assistance was required in only a cursory way.

AS IN EARLIER years, it was extremely helpful to create a chart to provide inspiration and focus for my homeschooling goals. I initiated the use of this chart in moments when the children appeared to be in need of stimulation. It gave us direction, facilitated motivation, and also provided a means to launch interesting subject matter. It usually turned out that almost half our weekly goals were met without my intervention and would simply be initiated spontaneously by the children.

Weekly Nautical Chart: Ages Seven and Eight

WNC: 7-8	1	2	3	4	5	6	7	8	9	10	11	12	13	14	15	16	17	18	19	20	21	22	23	24	25	26	27	28	29	30	31	32	33	34	35	36
Week																																				
Athletic Programs																																				
Baking																																				
Calendar–Moons, B'days,																																				
Computer Time																																				
Crafts																																				
Freestyle Painting																																				
Household Chores/Garden																																				
Math– Writing 1–50 to 1000																																				
Mathematics Games																																				
Mathematics Profile																																				
Math Times Tables 1–12																																				
Mixed Operations																																				
Music Appreciation																																				
Nature Hike																																				
Outside Time																																				
Paragraph and Illust.																																				
Paragraph and Illust.																																				
Reading Aloud Practice																																				
Reading Aloud Practice																																				
Reading Aloud Practice																																				
Science Profile																																				
Singing and Poetry																																				
Social Studies Profile																																				
Story-time																																				
Story-time																																				
Story-time																																				
Wellness Profile																																				
Landmark Fieldtrips																																				
Scrapbooks																																				
1st Tri.–Cons.Pair.Games																																				
2nd Tri.–ReadingGames																																				
3rd Tri.–Vowel/Cons.Games																																				

STORY-TIME REMAINED a deeply entrenched and vital aspect of our homeschooling journey. Because a child of this age is entering a time of heightened emotional responses—i.e. the feeling realm—stories began to hold a more powerful appeal. A child will not only observe the plot and the characters of a story at this age but will feel the emotions more fully and with deeper clarity. Language Arts began to take on a more sophisticated turn.

Due to a child's growing autonomy in reading and their enhanced level of comprehension, care must be taken in selecting age-appropriate literature. A child this age wants to be able to choose books independently, so it is important to provide suitable choices. I made a conscious effort to expose the children to a variety of styles in literature, but a child's preferences must be respected as well.

In addition to the authors enjoyed in previous years, many other authors' work entered our home library during this year.

Supplementary List of Authors—Ages Seven and Eight

- A. A. Milne
- Bill Peet
- Hugh Lofting
- Janell Cannon
- Kenneth Grahame
- Laura Ingalls Wilder
- Michael Bond
- Rudyard Kipling

To supplement the various fairy tales and other classic stories enjoyed in our home, I introduced many of Aesop's Fables, being careful to select gentle, age appropriate tellings. What follows is a list of fables that the children particularly enjoyed.

List of Aesop's Fables—Ages Seven and Eight

- A Wolf in Sheep's Clothing
- The Ant and the Grasshopper
- The Bat, the Bramble and the Cormorant
- The Boy Who Cried Wolf
- The City Mouse and the Country Mouse

- The Dog and the Bone
- The Dove and the Ant
- The Fox and the Billy-Goat
- The Fox and the Crow
- The Fox and the Grapes
- The Fox and the Stork
- The Fox Who Lost his Tail
- The Frog and the Ox
- The Greedy Weasel
- The Hen Who Laid Golden Eggs
- The Heron and the Fish
- The Horse and the Donkey
- The Jackdaw and the Pigeons
- The Lion and the Gnat
- The Lion and the Mouse
- The Milkmaid and Her Pail
- The Monkey and the Cat
- The Monkey and the Leopard
- The Oak and the Reed
- The Tortoise and the Hare
- The Traveller and the Bear
- The Two Donkeys and the Loads of Salt and Sponges
- The Two Pots
- The Two Stubborn Goats
- The Weasel and the Bunny-Rabbit
- The Wolf and the Crane
- The Wolf and the Dog
- The Wolf and the Lamb
- The Wolf, the Nanny-Goat, and the Kid
- Who Will Bell the Cat?

As before, the charts that I have provided act solely as guides and are not to be taken as rigid schedules. It is with this in mind that I listed story-time three times on chart WNC: 7-8 to allow for those weeks when other obligations preclude it. Similarly, the listing of Reading Aloud Practice was limited to three times per week with each child reading at least three pages from their chosen reader (refer to list in a previous section). Some weeks we would read together seven days per week and other times only three days due to other commitments.

By incorporating games into our homeschooling mix, I hoped to promote conventional academics in a seamless and enduring manner. Consonant pairings and reading games (instructions provided in the previous section), were augmented periodically with variations on rules and with the addition of more complex designs.

Vowel and consonant games became yet another source of learning that furthered the children's level of comfort with the written word. Instructions for a vowel and consonants game are given below. It is a game similar to the Wheel of Fortune game on television where a player needs to determine the solution to a puzzle by guessing applicable letters. As an added benefit, it served to reinforce mathematics as well.

Vowel and Consonant Game—Ages Seven and Eight

- The object of the game is to earn money by spinning a wheel and solving a succession of word puzzles. The player with the most money after four (or so) rounds is the winner.
- Construct a wheel out of sturdy construction paper and fasten an arrow-shaped spinner to the centre of the wheel.
- Divide the wheel into numerous pie sections, assigning dollar amounts to each. Keep the dollar amounts within the players' mathematical comfort levels.
- Create a list of various topics for solving. Suggestions for topics include: rooms in a home, animals in Africa, colours, foods, etc.
- Make play money using various colours of construction paper. Keep denominations small until child can manage larger amounts.
- Determine how much vowels will be worth, based on the players' ability.
- Choose words relating to the topics. Keep it simple at first, increasing difficulty level as players gain ability.
- Have the first player choose a topic and on paper or chalk/white board, give each letter in the answer one dash stroke, similar to the game Hangman.
- That player then spins the spinner.
- When the spinner stops on a dollar amount, the player can then guess a consonant. If the letter selected is in the puzzle, the player receives the dollar amount indicated by the spinner. If the letter appears in the puzzle more than once, the dollar amount is multiplied by the number of times the letter appears. The player continues to

spin and ask for letters until they choose a letter not present in the answer. Then it is the next players turn to spin.

- A player may buy a vowel during their turn provided they have enough money. If the vowel does appear, the player continues. If the vowel does not appear, the player ends their turn.
- During any of their turns, a player may elect to solve the puzzle.
  - Tip: When children of different abilities are playing, it is often necessary to alter the rules for the game to remain fair and appealing. For example, for a less capable player, more than one letter may be chosen at one time, the dollar amount awarded for correct letters may be doubled, etc.

Even though our world has largely been inundated with keyboards and computer screens, I feel that it remains essential to communicate well with pen and paper. However, encouraging my children to practice writing at this age is frequently a challenge. A child is often too preoccupied with applied living to slow down long enough to reflect on the exact form of letters and placing their thoughts on paper, so it was necessary to come up with more enticing methods. I supported their correspondence with pen-pals, as well as the making of lists, silly creative writing books, calendars, their own readers, etc. The goal of these pursuits was to facilitate comfort in penmanship. With the addition of two paragraphs with illustrations as a goal on my chart, I hoped to support a habit of writing. In practice, their efforts were technically not in paragraph form; however, their handwriting practice remained valid.

As in previous years, I maintained scrapbooks for the children's creative projects and supported their efforts to decorate the borders, encouraging them to use a continuous line if possible. This was a pleasurable diversion for the children but once their enthusiasm waned, we filed their scrapbooks away for another day. I wanted the children to enjoy their creative expression and not become weary or frustrated with penmanship. Again, I felt that the process was more important than the build-up of layers.

MATHEMATICS FOR THIS age group assumes more importance and must be pursued actively but still with a sense of light-heartedness. The reliance on games and tangible objects to promote knowledge of mixed operations remained a priority, with worksheets set at a minimum.

Instructions for a mathematics game are located in the previous section but for this age group it may be wise to supplement with multiplication. I introduced a new times table to the children every two weeks or so and at that time added it into existing games. I supported their efforts with gentle guidance, always aware of the importance of process over end results. We performed as a collaborative group and achievement was acknowledged and celebrated.

I also maintained the incorporation of storytelling into mathematics practice. For instance, when we discussed place value, by utilizing the Internet (websites provided at the back of this book), I was able to locate a story that I could fine-tune to present a more attractive notion for the children. I felt that through this story, the children would be able to reap a finer appreciation of the concept. This story is presented below.

Place Value Story—Ages Seven and Eight

> Once upon a time, there was an exceptionally undersized castle owned by a gracious but poor man named One. His castle could only shelter nine knights in total. Whenever an occasion arose where more than nine knights required lodging, the remaining knights were obliged to be boarded with One's cousin, Ten, at the neighbouring castle. Ten had a larger castle and could accommodate 90 knights in all. When a particular large celebration attracted even more knights, they found accommodation at yet another cousin's castle. This castle was owned by Hundred and could lodge 900 knights. At a crowning or any other tremendously special gala, when even more knights were gathered, the additional knights could be housed by a cousin named Thousand, who lived across the river Comma.

This story demonstrates place value in very simple terms and I found that the children were able to fully grasp the model.

In addition, I encouraged the children to write out a selected times table and a set of fifty numbers per week. After some practice, the children became comfortable with the patterns inherent in numbers and gladly noted their own achievements.

To supplement these topics, I produced a profile for mathematics. I have provided it below for interest's sake.

Mathematics Profile—Ages Seven and Eight

- Conduct experiments comparing lighter and heavier.
- Consider ordinal numbers using tangible objects (i.e. first, second, third).
- Discuss place value through the story given above.
- Gather change and practice counting money to one dollar.
- Make a graph depicting a topic of the children's choosing (i.e. the number of children in the homes of friends, the number of friends with blonde hair, brown hair, red hair and black hair, etc.).
- Produce a worksheet for sequencing to 99 with eight spaces missing.
- Spend time jointly composing stories to promote basic mathematics skills.
- Use tangible objects to illustrate greater than and less than between the numbers zero and 99.

THE LINK BETWEEN a child's natural rhythms and the routines in their daily life remains important. A child's sense of well-being and control is heightened when they can predict their week. The constant repetition of their daily habits can seem slightly maddening to us, but it offers them the chance to take some control of their lives. Without rule and harmony, too much spontaneity can occur and this may cause both anxiety and stress. By this age, contributing to weekly household maintenance, baking, gardening, athletic programs, daily outdoor time, healthy eating habits, and regular exercise should be a customary part of a child's life.

Again, to enhance the children's health education, I felt it was useful to create a Wellness Profile. The one I used during this year is provided below for reference.

Wellness Profile—Ages Seven and Eight

- Discuss the following:
- Car safety and spend time play-acting with the children's bikes, cars, etc.
- Each family member's chores or duties within the family.
- How a family takes care of itself, animals, environment, etc.

- The concept of electricity and have the children consider safety issues.
- What happens within your body when sick.
- What to do in a case of fire. Hold a fire drill.
- Examine different facial expression found in magazines and in the mirror and imagine what the individual is feeling.
- Experiment with bike reflectors and flashlights. Look at shadows and how they are formed.
- Experiment with loud and soft sounds. Discuss vibrations.
- Go for a hearing exam. Have the children consider how you hear and how balance is related to the ear.
- Go for a walk in the rain and discuss the importance of appropriate clothing.
- Look at a family photo album and observe how each family member's hair has changed over the years.
- Observe animal teeth and why they are shaped the way they are.
- Plan a field trip to a mechanics shop.
- Play charades acting out various foods. Discuss what happens to food once it enters your body.
- Play spa. Have the children soak their feet in warm water and lavender essential oil.
- Play store and pay for merchandise using cash, coin, debit card, cheque and credit card.
- Practice gymnastics, yoga, stretching and bending.
- Put on a talent show.
- Study various spices in a spice rack and discuss where they come from.
- Take a census. Encourage the children to decide on the topic (i.e. do you like big dogs or small dogs, what is your favourite colour, etc.).
- Trace the children's bodies on a large sheet of paper and have children colour clothing on their sketches.
- Travel to a gardening centre and examine soil, fertilizer, compost, etc. and discuss the life and death of plants.
- Visit a fire hall.
- Where are we in the world? (Address, province, country, hemisphere). Have children attempt to memorize their own address and phone number.

DISAPPEARING FOR A hike in nature—be it through the woods, or to a beach, a park or a river—can offer a respite from the noise in today's world. Welcoming these diversions enhances our experiences and promotes a reverence for nature's beauty. It is for these reasons that a weekly nature hike with our well-loved dog remains a favourite activity and a necessary part of our homeschooling passage through this age.

As in previous years, I fashioned a Science Profile to further enhance our regular voyages into the natural world and to promote meaningful discovery.

Science Profile—Ages Seven and Eight

- Establish a seasonal table and modify it as each season passes. Discuss what makes the seasons happen.
- Create calendars for the children to fill out and decorate with each passing month.
- Compose a story about a garden in winter and the dreams of seeds.
- Create a story about a duck at his summer home.
- Discuss how humans help animals.
- Discuss plants and animals as food.
- Go for a drive and compare rural and urban areas.
- Discuss various forms of transportation.
- Discuss the various jobs an animal may have.
- Have the children consider what the earth is made of.
- Play games using the five senses (blindfold games, hearing tests, taste tests, etc.).
- Play with beeswax and mould it into various animals.
- Visit an observatory and discuss planets, stars and moons.
- Visit the local library and borrow books pertaining to the following:
  - Amphibians. Discuss how they differ from other animals.
  - Reptiles. Contrast them with amphibians.
  - Desert animals. Discuss how they have adapted to their harsh environment.
  - Insects.
  - Fish. Visit a local pet store and observe a variety of fish.
  - Birds. Search the Internet researching a favourite bird. Go bird watching.
  - Mammals. Play charades acting out a variety of species.
  - Animal behaviour.

- How animals communicate.
- Natural resources.

TO FURTHER THEIR awareness of the history of the land around us, each month I would suggest to the children that we visit one of the many geographical landmarks in our area. This was a superb means to venture away from our regular practices while discovering the surrounding region. We would often invite the local homeschooling community to participate with us and this provided many happy memories, furthering the children's sense of ownership of their community.

It is a common belief in many halls of traditional education that it is prudent to teach the telling of time to this age group. I did not however, endeavour to introduce this concept at this age primarily due to the children's lack of interest, choosing instead to facilitate awareness of time in a less direct sense. I encouraged the children to appreciate the gentle passing of time through appreciation of the seasons. We produced calendars to mark the various months noting important dates like holidays, birthdays, anniversaries and full moons and welcomed each season with the changing of our seasonal table and various traditions that we had established over the years.

Participating in weekly nature and seasonal crafts and spending time sculpting clay creations remained a vital element in our home-schooling venture. While the supply cupboard in our homeschool "class-room" had long been established and had always been maintained and replenished, it became necessary to acquire even more advanced project books to promote further inspiration.

Painting was another much loved activity that continued from previous years. It remained a self-directed pursuit but acquiring art books with inspiring projects enriched this endeavour. My participation was welcomed and often still served as a catalyst for the children's involvement.

On quite a different note, the use of the computer continued to play a part, albeit a minor one, in our homeschooling week. Its use was still limited to a half-hour per week. As before, computer software was carefully chosen for its educational value and for age-appropriateness. The children's sessions went largely unsupervised and I gave assistance only when asked. The only exception to this was when the children requested the use of the internet. This activity was always faithfully monitored. Since we rarely promoted television viewing, it also remained an insignificant part of our lives. During these years, we occasionally watched a movie on the weekends, but that was a rare occurrence. My objective was to promote active minds and a healthy lifestyle, and excessive television viewing worked contrary to that outcome.

We continued to enjoy weekly singing as a family. This was often initiated by my own impromptu crooning of many of the songs listed in previous sections.

To further enrich our auditory homeschooling experience, the children and I regularly read aloud poetry of various styles. To maintain a deep level of interest in poems, it was necessary to acquire an assortment of stimulating poetry anthologies for the children. They would choose their favourites and this led to many pleasurable afternoons. Our early forays into composing poetry were fun-filled and silly, for again, process was far more prized than final product.

Since my husband and I are both musical, we enjoy peppering our daily lives with various musical forms. As a result, our children love a range of music. Weekly guitar playing was part of our routine, fashioned by encouraging the children's hands-on experiments and messing around. I did not teach the children to play the guitar at this age but simply supported their efforts, hoping to promote their complete comfort with the instrument and a love for its sound potential. The children remained content to merely engage in instrumental shenanigans and I was happy to lead the band.

AS THIS YEAR proceeds, a child changes enormously. They appear to progress from a fairly dependent individual to one that requires outside friendships and autonomy in nearly every decision. They are acquiring more knowledge every day and are striving for self-sufficiency. They can be rebellious yet still require a parent's support, understanding, respect, and cooperation. A parent's influence remains great and within a parent's love, a child will learn best.

AGAIN WITH THE intent to further clarify the above discussion, I have provided below a portrayal of two typical days in our homeschooling journey when the children were ages seven and eight.

Captain's Logbook—Ages Seven and Eight

Monday morning arrives and as my husband retrieves the newspaper from the only puddle found on our driveway, I challenge myself to make cappuccinos. The children remain in bed, blissful unaware and my husband and I enjoy quiet, early morning solitude.

In a bit of a stupor, I gradually detect two sets of twinkling, spying eyes, one set brown, one set blue, and make an effort to appear like I have not noticed. I feign interest in the newspaper and the children exclaim in what is meant to illicit a frightening jolt. My husband, genuinely astonished, nearly spills his coffee! The children race in for hugs and kisses and promptly demand breakfast! I reply, "Excuse Me?" and before long we are back on track and I help the children prepare their own breakfast.

As breakfast dishes are unceremoniously hurled into the dishwasher, I take a moment to peruse the day's plan in my calendar. It appears that our only genuine commitment is an afternoon walk with the local homeschooling group. I travel to the shower noting as I do that the children have retired to their respective rooms, pursuing their own projects. I suggest the children make plans to get ready for our day as I take my own advice.

As the morning routine is completed, I enterprise to make lemonade from scratch. The children delight in my idea and as lemons are squeezed and the juice is drunk, we take note of their homemade calendars and consider what events will take place over the next two weeks.

Halloween approaches, so we make plans to organize a field trip to a neighbourhood pumpkin patch and corn maze. It happens to be situated on a heritage farm. I consider the possibilities and make a few requisite phone calls.

After my attention is directed back to the children, we consult our arts and crafts books for ideas on decorating for this year's spooky eve. Before we know it, most of the morning is consumed in scary adornments and sticky goop.

As the children fatigue of this activity, I select a familiar compact disk and we march around the house, singing our choice songs and delighting in silly dances. My daughter suggests we supplement this occasion with guitars and the experience becomes increasingly boisterous. The children are content to mess around with their instruments and are quite elated with our symphony. The compact disk energetically draws to an end and we gather on the couch to read some of our favourite poems.

We take turns reading our most preferred selections and many choices not yet sampled. Feeling uncertain as to what to suggest next, I consult the Wellness Profile for this homeschooling year and entice the children to follow me to the kitchen.

I open the spice cabinet and proceed to open jars, allowing the children to sample as they see fit. We discuss the origins of many of them but before long, my son grows weary of this activity, and suggests we all play a board game.

We assemble around the kitchen table, my son taking complete control of the game. While the children are preoccupied, I elect to make a lunch unassisted. While a pot of soup is simmering on the stove, I realize I have not updated their mathematics cards for quite some time.

We no longer use dice for our assortment of board games and instead use cards emblazed with numbers and the signs for plus, minus and times. I promptly cut out a few cards out of construction paper and add the three times table to their stack. I take a few minutes to sit with the children to offer any assistance necessary and answer a couple of phone calls in the process.

As I ladle out our vegetable soup, the children and I discuss our afternoon adventure. We are to meet the local homeschooling group at the parking lot of a local lake and hike together along the forest path that leads to its shores. We have never been to this lake and are thoroughly anticipating new discoveries. As we look out the window, we hope for fair weather on this unpredictable west coast of Canada.

After lunch dishes are cleared, we pack entirely too many supplies for one afternoon at a lake and pile in the car. We hope to arrive at the lake with plenty of time to explore on our own before the rest of the assembly arrives. We are greeted at the parking lot by a few other homeschooling families who apparently had the same notion. We happily greet our friends and introduce ourselves to the obvious newcomers. As the parents leisurely amble toward the lake through the rainforest-like beauty, the children race in their own oblivious resplendence.

We finally land at the lake after a fifteen minute walk and are greeted by the shouts of our children, happily playing tag. They are a mixed group of children, aged thirteen to four, heartily playing together as a pack. Many of them have known each other for several years and the newcomers have apparently been welcomed seamlessly into their network.

We parents enjoy these outings as much as the children for they present us with an opportunity to discuss our favourite topic—home-schooling! We discuss our successes, what our children are interested in and what approaches we use to engage our children and maintain motivation.

The weather has thus far cooperated but as it is getting late and a wind has picked up, we make preparations to depart en masse. To "Good-bye!" cheers and horns blaring, the children and I reflect on the day and travel home weary but contented. Surprisingly, we arrive home in tandem with Daddy.

I heat up leftovers for supper and afterwards, my husband settles on the couch to read to the children. I take this opportunity to create some semblance of order in the kitchen and as bedtime approaches, I suggest to the children that they journey to the bathtub and make ready for lights out. As the curtain drops on the children's day, my husband and I anticipate a quite night of writing, bookkeeping, reading and listening to music.

Tuesday morning we unwittingly oversleep. My husband, in distress, races to work, obligatorily forgetting his lunch. I am prickly and irritable, but finally manage to break a smile when the children surprise me with the ridiculous costume they have wrestled our ever-willing dog into. I must now refer to him as our beloved bumble bee!

Today is "wash clothes" day, so directly after a slapdash breakfast, we tidy up the dishes and sort the dirty clothes. I decide to forgo a shower and start our hiccupping washer instead.

Before long, I am unceremoniously summoned to my daughter's room in order to extract her brother from her room, "in no uncertain terms," she declares.

I know from experience that to minimize interference in the daily interactions of siblings is most conducive to minimizing sibling rivalry. Often they can reach agreements on their own, albeit sometimes not as equitably as I would like, but still with the consent of both parties.

Today, being summoned in this way, informs me that they are unable to reach a compromise on their own and need my assistance. Careful to remain impartial, I listen to both sides affecting calm, and do my best to manage the tension. I ask open-ended questions and try to listen without judgment or blaming. We are able to negotiate an agreement and they grudgingly quiet down and pursue less antagonistic quests. Planning to distance the children from this episode, I suggest we set off for the grocery store with our two-page, jam-packed with fun, shopping list.

We succeed in arriving at the store in one congenial piece and proceed down the aisles, falling into familiar, well-oiled form. A torrential downpour commences as our grocery bags greet the great outdoors and celebrate by virtually disintegrating on the spot.

As we unpack our sopping provisions, we are all slightly annoyed at our shaggy headed dog with his nose in each and every bag in turn. I decide we all could use a respite, so instead of hurrying to tackle more laundry, I advocate for a story.

The children are thankful to sit down, relax and recuperate. We take turns reading passages from a wonderful book courtesy of A. A. Milne and feel much recovered, taking time to notice the rain letting up.

My son, in need of a diversion, travels to the kitchen to gather various painting supplies while my daughter requests a morning bath to ward off a chill that has begun to set in.

After my daughter's hot bath, she contracts a creative urge and decides to join in the painting fun while my son elects to have a bath. After all this has transpired, I move to the kitchen to prepare lunch, daydreaming of how magnificent a bath would feel.

We tidy the lunch dishes, note the time and fling all items necessary for the children's swimming lessons into our "has seen better days" backpack. We heave ourselves into the car, rechecking that we have everything.

The sky remains grey even though the rain has stopped, but before long we are wet again anyway! At least the pool water is warm—almost. The children advance to their lesson and receive their report cards on a job well done. They splash and yell with their friends and the hour passes rapidly. We celebrate the end of this swimming session with a sugary treat from a vending machine.

At home once more, I consult my chart and suggest to the children that we engage in mathematics exercises. When they grumble and protest, I gently remind them of their commitment to our basic homeschooling goals. They campaign for a reprieve until tomorrow so I make a note in my calendar to act as a reminder. I change gears and propose a consonant pairings game and their verve is revisited.

Immediately following our game, the children advance toward their self-led activities and I seize this chance to catch up on the laundry. They play contentedly for over an hour and emerge relaxed but famished. We make supper collectively, and my husband appears just as we are polishing off the benefits of our efforts! I swiftly reheat a plate for him and the evening unfolds without incident.

WE HAVE EXPANDED our perceptions during these days in a variety of ways but have remained firmly rooted in our family. We have accomplished our goals, sometimes miraculously, and followed our own paths to further self-determination. Our homeschooling was rooted on the principle that a parent must ensure a child's pursuit of deepest wishes, showing respect for their will and their awakening feelings and ultimately, providing them with an authentic childhood.

CHAPTER EIGHT—AGES EIGHT AND NINE

Nautical Compass—Ages Eight and Nine

Children in this age group are on the brink of adolescence and are becoming more resistant to parental influence and progressively more reliant on individuals outside the family for companionship. They are more apt to grumble and feel anxious and can be tremendously thoughtful and reserved at times. On other occasions, they can be truly animated and outright unruly.

Parenting a child of this age group can be demanding and home-schooling a child this age offers further challenges. A child's potentially unpredictable and often temperamental nature provides countless opportunities for a parent to re-evaluate their methods and parenting instincts. There appears to be a preconception in our society that there is a prescribed mode of behaviour for children and that it is a parent's duty to alter their children's conduct to correspond with this societal perception. However, this is nothing more than misplaced expectation.

As children of this age group shyly glimpse the next chapter of their lives, they develop an appreciation for their individuality and capabilities and an acceptance of who they are as unique persons. When they receive approval for their labours, they advance along their passage to selfhood. Personal progress and feelings of accomplishment do much to counteract most negative behavioural issues. Experience has shown me that it is only with complete acceptance and love for a child's intensity, that real change can occur in altering unconstructive expressions of a child's power. It is only when negative behaviours are allowed to surface that they can be worked through and transformed. This is not to suggest that foul, discourteous actions should be completely ignored, only that you must delve deeper to consider where the behaviour is rooted. When a parent sincerely accepts a child's vital spirit and deepest instincts, a genuine bond is established with them. In effect this empowers them to turn the page themselves.

When parenting this age group, it is especially important to maintain a fairly relaxed and flexible manner. Since any child-led activities tend to provide a child with their greatest pleasure, family harmony is more effectively promoted by encouraging a child's natural rhythms. Respect for a child's unique interests is important, not only for a successful home-schooling year but for the nurturing of a child's natural instincts.

Also, the nurtured ebb and flow of a homeschooling week will provide a certain level of comfort to a child who may be struggling with confused feelings and doubts. Confidence in your ability to rely on a predictable home environment creates the security necessary to grow and achieve well-being.

As a child matures, the need for a democratic commitment to ho-meschooling goals becomes as challenging as it is valuable. Littering a child's day with fresh ideas and enticing concepts provides little meaning if a child remains closed to foreign notions. Encouragement to stay open to new experiences promotes a partnership between parent and child on a journey towards present and future fulfillment.

Perhaps the most useful addition to this year of homeschooling is the active employment of a reasonable yet flexible routine to promote the accomplishment of academic goals. By creating a relaxed learning routine, a parent is freed from the uncomfortable situation of pressuring a child to participate. When children form a commitment with a parent to follow this learning routine, before long, many goals may be accomplished with minimal friction.

At ages eight and nine, a child's abilities are greatly surpassing their earlier efforts and their capacity for knowledge is increasing. By this age, children become better equipped to absorb information and are capable of more prolonged focus and concentration. With the benefit of their democratic commitment to their own education, I tried to introduce a more scholarly approach to their learning, especially regarding language and mathematics concepts but still maintaining a focus on celebrating their will and their awakened feelings.

AS IN PREVIOUS years, it was useful to generate a chart to provide suggestions for activities and to provide a focal point for our home-schooling year. This chart was used as a guide, aiding motivation while upholding a strong element of adaptability. It became a tool for initiating fresh subject matter—topics that could be embraced by the children immediately or postponed for another occasion.

Weekly Nautical Chart: Ages Eight and Nine

WNC: 8-9	1	2	3	4	5	6	7	8	9	10	11	12	13	14	15	16	17	18	19	20	21	22	23	24	25	26	27	28	29	30	31	32	33	34	35	36
Week																																				
Athletic Programs																																				
Calendar-Moons, B'Days,																																				
Computer Time																																				
Creative Projects																																				
Freestyle Art Projects																																				
Games																																				
Games																																				
Games																																				
Handwriting																																				
Handwriting																																				
Handwriting																																				
Chores/Gardening																																				
Math/L.Arts/S.Stud. Sheets																																				
Math/L.Arts/S.Stud. Sheets																																				
Math/L.Arts/S.Stud. Sheets																																				
Mathematics Profile																																				
Music Lesson/Practice																																				
Music Lesson/Practice																																				
Music Lesson/Practice																																				
Nature Hike																																				
Outside Time																																				
Reading Aloud Practice																																				
Reading Aloud Practice																																				
Reading Aloud Practice																																				
Science Profile																																				
Singing and Poetry																																				
Social Studies Profile																																				
Spelling																																				
Spelling																																				
Spelling																																				
Wellness Profile																																				
Visit Historical Sites																																				
Scrapbooks																																				

TO AUGMENT CHART WNC: 8-9, I created profiles for Wellness, Mathematics, Science and Social Studies. I also developed worksheet profiles for Mathematics and Language Arts. I planned to encourage elements of naturalness into our curriculum, so that we could move seamlessly from topic to topic without a feeling of artificiality. These profiles were to be offered in a relaxed manner, with a sense of spontaneity yet guided by mindfulness. With allowances for the children's essential individuality, subject matter was always presented with hopes for meaningful encounters.

The blending of a family's rhythms and customary daily routines remains an important element during this homeschooling year. A child's feeling of stress and nervous tension may be reduced with their ability to predict their weekly endeavours. Daily outdoor time, healthy eating habits and regular exercise combined with the routine of weekly home maintenance, sundry bookkeeping duties, baking, gardening, yard work and athletic programs, provide a healthful foundation.

To supplement the children's healthy lifestyle, I fashioned the following Wellness Profile for this age. It was intended to provide the children with an educational plan tailor-made to follow their particular interests. Others may find different ideas more suitable for use with their own children.

Wellness Profile—Ages Eight and Nine

- Assemble a board game and invent some new rules for it.
- Disassemble various household objects like flashlights and tape recorders and try to put them back together.
- Discuss the following:
    - All the different types of homes that may be found in a city.
    - Recycling and why it is important to the planet.
    - Road safety.
    - The various foods the children enjoy. Where those foods originate and when they come into season.
    - What protects us from harm?
    - What safety measures are taken to help prevent a house fire? Formulate a plan in case of a fire and stage a fire drill.
- Gather the different types of belts that can be found in the home.
- Gather various objects that glow in the dark and play hide and seek with them in a darkened room.

- Give a pet a bath.
- Go for a picnic.
- Have the children construct a poster of their favourite things.
- Look at germs under a microscope.
- Make an indoors obstacle course.
- Make homemade stuffed animals and try to repair broken toys.
- Plan various field-trips. Visiting places of work that have already been encountered is quite alright since as a child ages, different aspects will likely make an impact.
- Prepare a snack together and discuss the importance of hygiene.
- Remember friends or relatives that have moved away.
- Visit a cemetery.
- Visit the local library and borrow children's books pertaining to the human body.
- Visit the local library to borrow children's books concerning adoption and discuss different kinds of families.

OUR FREQUENT NATURE hikes through forests or along beaches offered a welcome reprieve from our customary activities. And as always, our dog enjoyed these too. As in previous years, I shaped a Science Profile to provide further meaning to our standard excursions into nature. It is offered below for interest's sake.

Science Profile—Ages Eight and Nine

- Establish a seasonal table and update it with each passing season.
- Conduct experiments to observe the three states of water: gas, liquid, and solid.
- Discuss the following:
    - A variety of locations where you can find water and consider that there is only a finite amount of water on earth.
    - Gravity. Compose a story about it.
    - How humans and animals are interdependent.
    - Lightning and thunder storms.
    - Photosynthesis.
    - The different layers of atmosphere.
    - The different types of climate while looking at a map of the world.

- Which animals have back bones and which do not? Discuss the role of a skeleton and what happens when a bone is broken.
- List various natural resources.
- Introduce the children to the concept of a cell.
- On a nature hike, observe the following:
  - Clouds, and try to predict the weather.
  - Plants which have a stem and those without.
  - The terrain.
  - Different types of water bodies.
- Make a chart to note the types of clouds present, temperature, precipitation, wind direction and air pressure over the span of a few weeks.
- Visit a local library and borrow books concerning the following:
  - Caves. Discuss the difference between stalactites and stalagmites.
  - Endangered animals and their protection.
  - Sea life.
  - Earthquakes and volcanoes.
  - Mountains and mountain climbing.
  - The north and south Polar Regions.
  - Different classes of rocks.
  - The jungles of the world.

IN THE PRECEDING year, we ventured into our district and visited neighbouring geographical landmarks garnering a sense of the local landscape. During this homeschooling year, we decided to focus on our area's history by visiting various community museums, historic homes and displays. We did this on a monthly basis and took photographs to document our travels and created many significant memories. Back at home, we created small books where the children could place their favourite photographs from our excursions and compose a few sentences about their learning encounters. This was a wonderfully expressive means to revisit our experiences and discuss what we harvested from each tour.

To complement these forays into our community, I created a Social Studies Profile that was directed by my children's interests. Again, since all families are unique, it may be necessary to include other, more precise subject matter to provide meaningful discoveries for your family.

Social Studies Profile—Ages Eight and Nine

- Discuss an assortment of occupations.
- Discuss different forms of communication and contrast them with how the animal world communicates.
- Discuss various ethnic groups.
- Make a map book and over the next few weeks, have children demonstrate how to get to a friends home, how to get around your own yard, how to get to the grocery store, how to get around your home, how to get around your own room, etc.
- Make a sundial and observe it through the course of a day.
- Observe the sun's position at various times per day.
- Review the days of the week.
- Review the months of the year.
- In conference with the children, we decided to turn our focus more to the study of Canada. We borrowed books from the library that provided background information so children could answer the following questions:
  - By land mass, where does Canada rank in the world? Is Canada the world's largest country?
  - How many territories are there in Canada?
  - How many time zones are there in Canada?
  - How many provinces are there in Canada?
  - What is Canada's national animal?
  - What animals, people or things are depicted on Canadian money?
  - What are Canada's natural resources and where are they found?
  - What are Canada's official national languages?
  - What are the names of the provinces and territories?
  - What are the capital cities of each province?
  - What are the regions of Canada and what is their climate like?
  - What countries border Canada?
  - What is Canada's largest territory?
  - What is Canada's smallest province?
  - What is considered Canada's national sport?
  - What is the capital city of Canada and in what province is it found?
  - What is the highest mountain in Canada and in what province can it be found?

- What is the leader of Canada called?
- What is the Canadian national anthem?
- What is the origin of the name "Canada"?
- What kind of leaf is at the centre of the Canadian flag?
- What standard of measurement is used to record temperature in Canada?
- What oceans touch Canada?
- What province do we live in?
- What was the name given to the system of safe houses that allowed American slaves to reach freedom in Canada?
- Where is Canada?
- Which province was last to join Confederation?
- Which territory was most recently formed and when?
- Who led the Métis in the rebellions at Red River in the northwest in the 1800s?
- Who was Laura Secord and what is she famous for?
- Who was the first Canadian Prime Minister?
- Who were the first people to live in Canada?
- Who is the Prime Minister of Canada?

I ALSO PRODUCED a Mathematics Profile for the children during this homeschooling year. My intent was to employ these topics throughout the year in as natural and meaningful a manner as possible. I strove to be alert for opportunities to enhance their real world learning with focused attention on practical mathematical concepts. The profile is offered for perusal.

Mathematics Profile—Ages Eight and Nine

- Over several weeks, have children write down numbers from 1 to 10,000. To make this a less arduous task, have children write the first 100 numbers and then write the rest of the numbers counting by 100's (i.e. 99, 100, 200, 300, etc.).
- Introduce Roman numerals to XX.
- Make a bar graph, measuring and weighing a variety of objects like toys, books, balls, etc.
- Review the concepts of plus, minus, times and divide, utilizing tangible objects in a variety of games.
- Sort coins and practice counting money of various denominations.

BY RESEARCHING THE Internet, I created worksheets for Mathematics and Language Arts. These were designed to present the children with a basic understanding of standard principles and data. I achieved a commitment from the children of one page per day with the understanding that flexibility was entirely welcomed. The children were given absolute discretion each day on the choice of pages completed and I retained permission to ensure basic understanding of the concepts presented. I commended their efforts and considered their work gently. The children were encouraged to complete as many pages in a day as they desired.

These worksheets were meant to provide the children with practice in achieving new skills but special efforts were made to ensure personalized parameters were firmly in place. I sought to guarantee that the children never felt overwhelmed or mired in excessive "homework" as sometimes may occur with the seemingly endless repetition of skills already mastered. I strove to provide my children with essential skills while avoiding the discouragement that can come from too much repetition and learning by rote. I did this to ensure their continued dedication to their own education and to preserve their enjoyment of the subject matter.

With the help of a flexible routine, many of our homeschooling goals were completed without incident. The best illustration of this was the completion of worksheets. Following their morning custom of brushing teeth, combing hair, getting dressed and making beds, it became routine for the children to automatically rush back downstairs to complete their worksheet commitment. This activity was rarely postponed and once their day's worksheet was completed, they seemed to feel a genuine sense of accomplishment.

Below are the worksheet profiles that I created for the children during this homeschooling year.

Mathematics Worksheet Profile—Ages Eight and Nine

- Eight worksheets for addition and subtraction practice using numbers between zero and 100. Allocate 25 questions for each worksheet.
- Two worksheets for practicing division with integer answers using divisors between one and five. Allocate 25 questions for each worksheet.

- Two worksheets for practicing division with remainders using divisors:
  - Between one and five. Allocate 25 questions for each worksheet.
  - Between six and ten. Allocate 25 questions for the worksheet.
  - Of 11 and 12. Allocate 25 questions for each worksheet.
- Five worksheets for practicing division with remainders using divisors between one and ten. Allocate 25 questions for each worksheet.
- Two worksheet for practicing multiplication problems using the:
  - Three and four times table up to the number 12. Allocate 20 questions for the worksheet.
  - Five and six times table up to the number 12. Allocate 20 questions for the worksheet.
  - Seven times table up to the number 12. Allocate 20 questions for the worksheet.
  - Eight times table up to the number 12. Allocate 20 questions for each worksheet.
  - Nine times table up to the number 12. Allocate 20 questions for each worksheet.
  - 11 times table up to number 12. Allocate 20 questions for each worksheet.
  - 12 times table up to the number 12. Allocate 20 questions for each worksheet.
- Ten worksheets for practicing multiplication problems using the zero to 12 times tables up to the number 12. Allocate 20 questions for each worksheet.
- Two worksheets for practicing place value up to 1000. Allocate 20 questions for each worksheet.
- Two worksheets for practice with greater than, less than and equal up to 1000. Allocate 20 questions for each worksheet.
- One worksheet for practicing multiplication using numbers between one and 20, utilizing a vertical format with carrying. Allocate 25 questions for the worksheet.
- One worksheet for practicing place value up to one million. Allocate 30 questions for the worksheet.

Language Arts Worksheet Profile—Ages Eight and Nine

- Provide the children with five worksheets for practice in spotting capitalization errors. Allocate ten questions for each worksheet.

- Provide the children with five worksheets for practice in spotting punctuation errors. Allocate ten questions for each worksheet.
- Provide the children with two worksheets for practice in the following:
    - Identifying verbs. Allocate ten questions for each worksheet.
    - Identifying nouns. Allocate ten questions for each worksheet.
    - Identifying adjectives. Allocate ten questions for each worksheet.
    - Identifying adverbs. Allocate ten questions for each worksheet.
    - Comparing adjectives and adverbs. Allocate ten questions for each worksheet.
    - Comparing nouns, verbs and adjectives. Allocate ten questions for each worksheet.

WEEKLY SPELLING PRACTICE was also a commitment which became an integral aspect of our daily routine. To facilitate this exercise, I acquired simple address books for each child. Each day after their worksheets were completed, I would provide them with a minimum of five spelling words (more if requested) to be written under the appropriate first letter in their address books, thus creating their own personalized dictionaries. I would help them only when asked but was permitted to ensure the accuracy of their work. This morning routine became so habitual and automatic that delays were rare.

Supplied below is a list of words that I encouraged the children to spell during this homeschooling year. I provided them with approximately 15 words per week (three days with 5 words each day—see chart WNC: 8-9) depending on the ebb and flow of family and home life. Whatever list you use, special attention should be given to match the list closely to a child's ability, presenting the child with challenging words but still maintaining their level of confidence.

List of Spelling Words – Ages Eight and Nine (1 of 3)			
about	boxes	dance	friend
across	branches	dead	front
add	brave	desk	funny
afraid	bread	die	ghost
after	breakfast	dinner	gift
afternoon	bright	doctor	giraffe
again	brush	doesn't	glove
age	build	dollar	goat
ago	burn	don't	goes
air	buses	done	grades
almost	butter	door	grape
also	cage	drank	grew
angry	called	drawing	grinned
another	campfire	dream	group
anyone	can't	driving	grumpy
anything	candy	drum	guess
apple	care	eagle	gym
arm	carries	early	half
around	carry	ears	hammer
art	caught	easy	hang
asked	chain	everyone	happen
back	change	everything	having
baked	cheek	eyes	hear
balloon	cheese	face	heard
band	cherry	falling	heart
bark	chew	family	heavy
barn	child	far	hello
basket	circus	farm	helping
bath	city	feeding	here
bean	classes	feeling	hiding
bear	clay	fifty	high
because	clean	fight	hiked
before	clear	fine	himself
behind	climb	fingers	hole
better	close	finish	horn
bigger	cloud	first	horse
bike	clown	fishing	house
birds	color	flash	huge
birthday	coming	flew	hurt
blew	cook	flies	I'll
blind	copy	float	I'm
blow	corn	foil	I've
body	count	food	ice
boot	crack	forgot	ill
born	crawl	found	inches
bowl	crazy	freezer	ink

List of Spelling Words – Ages Eight and Nine (2 of 3)			
isn't	milk	quickly	shopping
it's	Monday	rabbit	short
joy	money	race	should
kept	more	racing	sight
key	morning	rack	singer
kick	most	rage	sitting
kiss	mouse	raised	size
kitten	mouth	rake	skate
knee	move	rang	skin
knew	near	really	skinned
knife	neck	riding	skip
knock	never	river	sky
knot	newspaper	roar	sledding
know	noise	rode	slept
lady	none	roll	slice
lamb	noon	rope	slid
lands	note	roses	sliding
large	now	row	small
laugh	oak	rubber	smart
law	odd	rule	smell
lay	oil	running	smile
leave	once	rush	smiling
left	other	sack	soap
less	our	sail	sock
letter	outside	sailed	soft
lie	own	sale	someone
life	page	same	something
lift	paint	sang	son
liked	pancakes	Saturday	song
liking	park	saved	sorry
line	past	school	sound
little	pay	scratch	speak
lived	peaches	scream	spell
load	penny	sea	spill
lose	picked	second	spoil
loud	picnic	seem	sport
love	piece	send	spread
lunch	pink	sent	spring
mark	pipe	serve	stairs
match	point	sew	stamp
maybe	pool	shall	stand
meal	prize	shape	star
meat	push	shelf	start
meet	put	shell	stepping
merry	queen	shiny	stick
might	quick	shirt	stone

List of Spelling Words – Ages Eight and Nine (3 of 3)			
stopped	Thursday	until	woman
straight	tight	used	won't
straw	tiny	very	wood
stream	tire	voice	word
street	today	wagging	wore
stretch	together	walk	work
string	told	wall	would
strong	too	wanting	wrap
suit	tooth	warm	write
summer	torn	wash	wrong
Sunday	touch	watching	wrote
tail	town	water	yard
tape	toy	we'll	year
taste	toys	Wednesday	yet
teacher	track	were	young
team	trade	where	your
tent	traded	while	you're
tenth	trash	whole	
that's	tries	wild	
these	trouble	window	
thick	True	wing	
thin	trunk	winter	
threw	trust	wipe	
thrill	Tuesday	without	
throw	turn	woke	

A SIGNIFICANT ADDITION to this homeschooling year was the introduction of cursive handwriting. This endeavour can be a fairly intimidating pursuit for a young child and I do recommend that it transpire only when a child shows genuine interest in acquiring this new skill. In our home, this process was approached cautiously, with special regard given to allowing the children to lead as much as possible. To begin with, I would ask the children what silly words they would like to learn to write. After a few weeks of practicing this exercise at least three days per week, we tackled silly sentences beginning with each of the letters of the alphabet in turn. As interest in this began to wane and aptitude improved, we practiced handwriting by writing the alphabet in continuous cursive form.

After determining that the children had a suitable grasp of the correct formation of letters, cursive handwriting was encouraged for other activities as well. For instance, I provided the children with small notebooks for each profile subject and challenged them to compose five-line paragraphs relating to their discoveries and experiences. The children were reasonably comfortable with this new form of expression and were eager to apply cursive handwriting to routine efforts such as spelling practice, on birthday cards, on suitable worksheet pages and in countless other activities. In addition to this, I provided the children with an ongoing supply of notebooks for their own private use.

MANY ACTIVITIES PURSUED in previous years continued to inspire us during this homeschooling year, but no activity was more rewarding for us than reading together. Since the children were moving into the feeling realm, the stories that we read together held a more sensitive and engrossing appeal. This pursuit was prompted by almost any break in activity and was met with enthusiasm by all. Chapter books were overwhelmingly devoured as we took turns reading aloud at least three pages at a time. With the children's growing maturity and their bedtime being deferred to around 9 p.m., more time was available for delighting in a good book. Extended nightly reading became an essential aspect of nearly every homeschooling day.

Due to our enthusiasm for reading, it was necessary to add new books to our homeschool library. I was persistent in my desire for quality literature and maintained an ongoing supply of new materials. I added collections of folk tales from around the world to enhance our reading pleasure and supplemented our library with more advanced literature.

While we still enjoyed many of the authors listed previously, below are a few more authors whose works were particularly appealing during this homeschooling year.

Supplementary List of Authors—Ages Eight and Nine

- Astrid Lindgren
- E. B. White
- L. Frank Baum
- J. M. Barrie

Our home library also required continuous updating in other subjects as well. Since the children were well versed in self-directed learning, it was necessary to update our bookshelves with a variety of subject matter that was age-appropriate yet challenging. What follows is a sampling of reference and other books that could be found on our shelves.

List of Books for Self-directed Learning—Ages Eight and Nine

- A wide variety of enticing books on the sciences and history.
- A spirited book on understanding your body and other health issues.
- Books containing directions for simple science experiments that use everyday household items.
- Good quality animal encyclopaedias.
- High quality books on the geography of our country as well as several up-to-date atlases.

Another enjoyable endeavour that crept into our nightly habit was the playing of a diverse assortment of games. We continued to play many of the games that we produced ourselves in previous years, but were careful to maintain interest through adding ever-increasing challenges as well as adding new store-bought, age appropriate games.

Yet another recurring activity over the years was guitar practice. By the time the children had reached this age, I began to take a somewhat more formal approach. The children were becoming interested in creating sounds that were more pleasing to the ear, and they showed a keen interest in learning to play guitar. Following their lead, I changed the process we'd followed in previous years and developed a simple method to advance their knowledge while simultaneously maintaining the pleasure they derived from playing.

The children would choose a straightforward song from one of our many music notation books and I would demonstrate the correct way to play it, showing them how to read the music on the page and the corresponding finger positioning. I would then have them practice the piece. This went smoothly for a time, but as their ability improved, they became increasingly uninterested in such overtly, rudimentary exercises. Democratically, we fashioned a new plan.

The children would select a more advanced song to play. They would practice it through once (I would only help when asked) and then they would play it for me three times, to the best of their ability. I would make suggestions and corrections when I witnessed a potentially regrettable habit being formed. Once this exercise was completed, they would pursue guitar playing at their leisure.

This exercise fit itself seamlessly into the rhythms of an average day, usually occurring either before or after the children's bath time. With the increased level of focus and amount of practice that began to emerge, their proficiency gained immediate ground.

As the children became more proficient with reading notes and time signatures, they created music books ripe with their own compositions. These occasionally contributed to their daily practice, supplementing the musical notation books we already owned.

During this homeschooling year, I did my best to expose the children to a more in-depth assortment of musical styles. Our family possesses a large collection of CD's and recordings that represent a range of musical styles. This year, I aimed to categorize this music into different groups and demonstrate various selections to the children, pointing out key elements. After this exposure, the children would periodically express their preferences and eventually, they assumed control of this exercise while they still sought out new favourites.

Some weeks, due to other obligations, the children were unable to fulfill their outlined daily commitments—Games, Music Lessons, Reading-Aloud Practice, Handwriting Practice, and the Mathematics/Language Arts Worksheets. To allow for these diversions, I only listed these activities three times on the chart.

We maintained the observance of the passing weeks, months, and seasons. Each week we consulted our calendars to determine what events or celebrations might require special preparation. We honoured monthly full moons by roasting marshmallows, updated our seasonal table to commemorate each season and prepared for birthdays, anniversaries and holidays by decorating the house and creating cards to be delivered.

Prior to this year, the children had exhibited little sign of being ready or interested in telling time so I had yielded to their lead. During this homeschooling year however, they began to show an interest in the various clocks in our home and especially the movement of hands. Since I always tried diligently to have the children guide my efforts, I welcomed this interest.

Many new concepts can be best introduced through story and illustration. Telling time was no exception. What follows is a story I found on the Internet but altered to provide more meaning for my children.

Telling Time Story—Ages Eight and Nine

Once upon a time there lived an elderly dragon couple who were very happy because they lived so near their 12 (hours on a clock) dragon children and their 60 (minutes on a clock) dragon grandchildren. The Opa dragon (minute hand) was very agile even in his old age and always liked to be on the move. His wife (hour hand), though still quite spry, enjoyed lingering and resting. Each dragon child was blessed with five children of their own.

This elderly couple derived great pleasure in visiting their dragon children in each of their respective homes. Because the Oma dragon enjoyed longer visits and the Opa dragon preferred to hurry along, visiting the 12 dragon children and the 60 dragon grandchildren was quite a challenge

The Opa dragon would visit the 12 houses in the same time that it took Oma dragon to visit only one house. (The Opa dragon repre-

sents the minute hand speeding along minute by minute, while the Oma dragon symbolizes the hour hand slowly lingering an hour at each house).
• Tip: Use an illustration or an old clock to help tell the story.

Since we continued to read poetry, do crafts and paint every week, continuous replenishment of supplies for our homeschool "classroom" was obligatory. Special attention was given to acquiring poetry anthologies for children that were fun and whimsical, books of nature and seasonal crafts that were both appealing and distinctive, and art idea books that were of excellent quality while still being stimulating and novel. With the children's growing independence, it was also necessary to ensure that the materials provided were age-appropriate and accessible for independent absorption.

Each week, we enjoyed sculpting projects that utilized clay or bread dough. I acquired healthful yet motivating children's cookbooks that provided nutritious and tasty recipes. I also purchased a stimulating book on fashioning clay creations. I encouraged the children to determine these activities since I hoped to enhance real joy in their efforts and a love of form.

Toward the end of this year, my husband assumed more homeschooling responsibilities and initiated basic woodworking for the family on weekends. The children particularly enjoyed this imaginative occupation and participated in a variety of projects, learning numerous carpentry techniques.

Over the years, the children's abilities have steadily improved, granting a sense of confidence to many endeavours. Mastering new computer software was no exception and became a welcome challenge and a diversion from the everyday. I continued to strive to find quality programs that offered opportunities for learning while maintaining enrichment levels. Although I realized these activities were beneficial, I still maintained relatively strict time limits on computer time and still restricted television viewing to about two hours per week.

AGES EIGHT AND nine are years of awakening and change. Children of this age are gradually abandoning more and more of their early childhood tendencies and are better able to tackle more complex notions. They have moved away from their hands on, movement centric phase and are shifting to a more sophisticated feelings stage. As parents, we are blessed to witness a hint of the young adults they will become. These children require our continued acceptance and unfailing support on their journey to discover their place in the world. Constancy of home and family life are necessary for flight. They need to lean on our faithful presence now so that in the future such leaning will become unnecessary.

BELOW IS AN account of two typical days during our homeschooling year when the children were ages eight and nine. Again, this description is intended to provide further explanation as to the process illustrated in the previous discussion.

Captain's Logbook—Ages Eight and Nine

Monday emerges in soupy fog, coincidently indoors and outside. We have felt in slight disharmony as of late and are greatly anticipating our holiday which starts in two weeks time. My husband has been working many long hours these last few months and undeniably feels a sense of being alienated from his own being. He requires a vacation more than anyone but one would never guess it from his demeanour. He remains positive and exuberant despite encroaching deadlines. The children are completely unaware of his stressful work life and tumble into our bed as 7:30 AM arrives.

My daughter has been working through various phases over the last four months. The first phase revolved around constant, almost debilitating worry. The next was the sullen "I want to be alone" phase and as recently as last week, we were practically overwhelmed with a continually complaining phase. The duration of these stages appeared to lessen as we maintained our levels of patience, compassion, respect and encouragement and we are all relieved to moving steadily toward calmer waters.

Thankful to be receiving familiar warm cuddles and enthusiastic kisses, I shake off my dreamy sleep and carefully move to the washroom. The children stampede down the stairs of our new home while my husband sees to our impatient dog. The kitchen table is set by the time I make it downstairs and I proceed to make myself a foamy cappuccino. The children put in their orders for breakfast and I ask them to gather the necessary supplies. I assist their efforts to make their own breakfasts and move to the table to read the morning paper.

Before long it is time to officially start the day and my husband travels upstairs to shower and get ready for work while I prepare his somewhat unimaginative lunch for the day. The children follow their Dad upstairs to complete their own morning routine. I consult my calendar for any commitments for the day and by the time I'm done, my husband has completed his shower and it is now my turn.

The children are happily engaged in their own activities when I emerge from the washroom. My daughter is contentedly reading a favourite novel and my son is practicing his guitar. I make our bed, prepare my own breakfast and enlist the children's help to tidy the kitchen.

Later, my daughter joins me at our shared desk and proceeds to rifle through her worksheet binder. She is busy choosing her daily worksheet when her brother arrives to select his own page. They eventually decide on what they feel are just the right pages. My daughter has chosen a worksheet pertaining to locating adverbs and my son has selected a page for multiplication practice. I answer the few questions they ask and check my email in the meantime.

My daughter is first to complete her selected worksheet so I to verify her answers, gently correcting only when absolutely necessary. She takes out her spelling book and I call out her five spelling words for the day. She has some difficulty with two words but I help her out and then she elects to practice her cursive handwriting. Meanwhile, my son completes his worksheet and I consider it carefully. My daughter completes her task and advances to the front room to carry on reading her novel while I continue the morning learning routine with her brother.

Once my son's handwriting practice is finalized for the day, I suggest we grab our painting supplies for some creative expression before the children's morning free skate at 10:30. With the materials gathered, we each decide to paint a variety of trees using blow painting, a method described in one of the children's numerous art ideas books. When this challenge is completed, I remember that it is my mother's birthday in a couple of days and the children make cards out of their drying compositions.

At close to 10:00, we proceed to the car en masse with helmets, warm mittens and skates. The children had been participating in skating lessons for many years up to this point and have developed sufficient proficiency to truly enjoy skating. But, as of this September, they no longer wished to pursue further instruction. I felt that they had certainly given their best efforts over the years so skating for sheer pleasure became our goal.

Once at the rink, we lace up our skates and head to the ice. I am pleased to recognize another homeschooling family and the hour passes in a blur of colourful scarves and slippery stops. We are fatigued and happy to be heading home. Upon opening our front door, my son announces his desire to prepare lunch.

He heaves a substantial cookbook from the shelf and takes a few minutes to deliberate his choice for lunch. After a few minutes of reflection, he selects a baked macaroni, cheese and peas recipe and we gather the necessary ingredients. I assist when required and my daughter joins in the fun.

While our meal is baking, my daughter suggests we bake some cheese filled bunny pastries, the recipe for which she spied in one of our seasonal crafts books. She retrieves the book and as I roll out the dough, the children fashion the bunnies. Before long, it becomes a practiced assembly line and as the timer sounds indicating that the macaroni is ready, the bunnies take their final journey into the oven.

After our array of cheesy lunch dishes are washed and put away, we pile into the car once more, this time with our slobbering, blissfully happy dog in the back seat. We are planning to meet the local homeschooling group at a nearby beach for a hike and picnic. We assemble in the parking lot amid wild greetings and excitement, and it begins to steadily drizzle. We take an impromptu consensus; we contrive to ignore the bad weather, and set off as a dampened but prepared, boisterous group.

The children, oblivious to the soaking, guide us through the woods and as we emerge from the trees, we witness the tireless splendour of the ocean and happily, the cessation of the rain. We spend the afternoon catching up with old friends and discussing our triumphs and anxieties in our homeschooling march while the children pursue sandy surprises.

Once appetites are pacified by our picnic snacks, we recognize that it is getting late and pack up for our journey back through the woods. We are weary from our afternoon escapade and it is a hushed ride home.

Unfortunately, our supper is consumed before my husband returns home. I warm up his plate and with the completion of that evening's dishes, the children travel upstairs to alternate between bath time and guitar practice.

It is my daughters turn to have her bath first so while I am conditioning her tangled mass of hair, her brother sits down and selects a piece of music for this evening's practice. He chooses a melodic German lullaby and I hear him plucking along well before I am beckoned.

I toss my daughters dirty clothes in the laundry hamper and seek out my son to better hear his efforts. As this year has advanced, the children's progress has astounded me. With ease, my son completes three performances of the song and carefully puts away the guitar and music for another day.

I inform my daughter that she has five minutes more of bath time and I travel to my closet to retrieve my own guitar to practice some old favourites. Before I realize it, fifteen minutes has transpired and my daughter emerges from her bath, pink, prune-like and squeaky clean.

Now it is my son's turn for a soapy bath and my daughter hastily changes into pyjamas and gathers her selected music and guitar. Soon, guitar practice and bath time are over for another day and rooms have been cursorily tidied and sorted.

We convene downstairs to continue our reading of a story about a Native American tribe of the 1800's. We pause from time to time to discuss how different life was back in the 19th century and marvel at the people's ingenuity and determination. We take turns reading five pages each.

We decide that we have sufficient time for one simple experiment before bedtime, so we advance to our kitchen counter with one of our experiment books, consuming a few minutes gathering the essential supplies. This evening's choice concerns the attributes of light and reflection and we are pleased when we discover that our newly made kaleidoscopes work beautifully.

It is after 9:00 PM when we tidy our chaos from the kitchen counter and the children's beds are beckoning. After hugs and kisses and half-hearted attempts at stalling, the children journey upstairs to brush their teeth and dream new dreams.

I remain seated for a few minutes, enjoying my freshly made tea and my abrupt solitude. Hearing my husband, at work in our home office, prompts me to move to my computer to continue my writing and the night passes quietly.

Tuesday arrives with the familiar din of hammering rain. As 9:00 o'clock approaches, I take up the phone to arrange a visit with friends for the afternoon. After an enjoyable conversation, I am pleased to announce that our long time friends will be visiting us at around 1:30 this afternoon. With the echoing of excited squeals, I suggest we do some marching and singing around the house. My son exclaims his assent while my daughter, somewhat less enthusiastic, agrees.

My son and I march around the house, singing loudly, and both wondering how my daughter can resist the power of this commotion. As the final song draw to a triumphant crescendo, my son and I take a moment to check our thumping pulses while my daughter pursues her own challenges. We are exhilarated, warmed, out of breath and ready for the day.

After the furor subsides, the children gradually move to their worksheets, spelling and handwriting practice. Upon their completion, we all feel a sense of achievement and travel to the couch for reading practice with our current selection.

The children are particularly enjoying this latest book and are learning a great deal about Native American tools and their ingenious devices. They are so inspired that they begin plotting how best to duplicate of these methods in real life.

Over the last few weeks, we have been diligently adding pages to our map books and consequently, today I propose we sketch a map that our friends would employ to travel from their own home to ours. As my daughter finalizes her last pain-staking details of her map, she announces her desire to head outside now that the rain has subsided. After little more than two minutes, her brother has the same notion and we travel out the door and into the awakening sunshine.

The children grab their battle-worn bikes and thrill with their seasoned wings, circling around and around and around again. I spend a few minutes inspecting my assortment of beleaguered plants and shrubs, daydreaming of spring blooms. As lunch time approaches, I journey inside to heat up some leftovers from last night's supper and bellow for the children when it is time to eat.

After lunch, we curl up in front of a fire, read a few folktales and then open *The Wizard of Oz* to the front page. We take turns reading but after some time, the children require a change of activity. We decide to tackle some projects from our seasonal crafts book and happily pass the hour absorbed in our own creations.

Our friends will arrive shortly, so we jointly clean up our mess, eager to return outdoors to offer greetings. Our friends arrive to howls of delight from two children and one eager dog. We advance inside in great pandemonium, the children impatient to share in fun and games while I plug in the kettle for tea. After catching up on what's new, my friend and I take a few minutes to reflect on how our lives have been transformed over the years.

We first met each other at a quarterly homeschooling support group meeting that she happened to be hosting. At this point, our family had yet to connect with the homeschooling community and this was our inaugural outing. We did not know what to expect and felt nervous about meeting so many new people. We arrived at her residence, noticing at least ten cars of assorted vintages. As we entered her yard, I could discern children's lively voices emanating from the backyard.

I rang the door bell and was met by a woman about my age, smiling like someone who was sure to become a life-long friend. She was (and is) about my height and weight, but with beautiful long brown hair. She wore a simple skirt and blouse and was surrounded by the fragrant smell of fresh baking and was holding a cup of what I suspected was tea. I quickly introduced myself and the rest of my family, stating rapidly that she and I had spoken briefly on the phone the week before.

Upon finally putting a face to her warm voice, I smiled to myself and felt instantly at ease. She escorted us into her small but equipped kitchen, making a special effort to make the children feel welcome. She explained that her children were very close in age to them and were playing in the backyard with the other young guests. She asked if they would like to join them and guided them gently to the back door.

By this time, my husband and I were fully aware of the boisterous sounds radiating from the living room. Our hostess returned shortly and we sat for a few minutes in her kitchen, enjoying a cup of tea and sharing stories.

Eventually, we made our way to the living room, introductions were made and the meeting officially began. We discussed why we chose to homeschool, what our current challenges were and the successes we obtained. There was a genuine feeling of affinity in that we all had one true thing in common, we took (and take) parenting and homeschooling very seriously.

Over on a visibly comfy couch sat a family of three, a mother and father like bookends with a small child between them. The mother smiled warmly at me and I glanced at her daughter sitting prettily beside her. She was (and is) a beautiful child with an angelic face framed by long, curly blond hair. She sported, a brightly floral print dress making her appear more like a flower fairy than a little girl. The woman's husband was skilfully taking responsibility for the little girl while his wife visited with new friends and old. I felt completely at ease in their midst.

As the discussion became more formally driven, I observed a diverse assortment of individuals from all walks of life, applying differing philosophies to their homeschooling journey but unwavering in their encouragement of others without judgments made.

As the evening gently slipped by, I was pleased to meet many of the other parent's children. They were of myriad ages, playing together well and apparently enjoying the unstructured fun. A few of the children stopped long enough to chat with me and they spoke with complete comfort and self-assurance. I did not know which parents they were with but felt confident that I would figure it all out in due time. I had happily discovered a group of parents who I instantly felt I could come to in times of confusion, regardless of my own personal homeschooling methods or philosophy.

As today's visit drew to a close, I hugged my friend warmly. Through all the phases of homeschooling, she has offered support to me and me to her. We call out "Good-bye!" and travel back into the house, feeling completely uplifted. Friends will do that sometimes.

The children are growing hungry, so I begin preparations for supper while my son decides to withdraw to his computer software. My husband arrives just as supper reaches the kitchen table and we all speak at once, recounting our respective days.

AS THE EVENING draws to a close, I take a few moments to reflect on the life we have chosen. I am astonished when I become conscious of how the passage of time has transformed our family and how unpredictable a life truly is. The children are embarking on their unique paths of self-discovery and are distinguishing themselves as individuals. They acknowledge their growing independence from us, their parents and are expanding their capabilities. This internal knowledge sometimes creates uncertainty and concern within children but by being met with safe occurrences, respect for all feelings, democracy, cooperation, tolerance and a good helping of love, they can be remarkably resourceful and resilient.

As our family gathers in our living room to bid farewell to another day, I take time to be absolutely present in the moment and voice my love to my family. My daughter is anxious to continue reading our novel, so I acquiesce, slowing getting lost in the book and find myself transported to the mind of a little girl lost in a glorious, magical world. It is beautiful, yes, but she is correct. There is no place like home.

CHAPTER NINE—PORT OF CALL

A car slowly approaches and the children screech in anticipation. Shaken out of my reverie, I make my way to my front door to welcome my long lost friend and her family.

I am living a lifestyle that presents a marked contrast to the style in which Julia's has unfolded. The question remains whether our relationship can survive, given the apparent divergences that exist.

I swing open the front door and she meets my greeting with a warm embrace. Our eyes are moist as we realize this meeting has been too long in coming.

Over the years, we have often spoken of visiting each other but life has always seemed to get in the way. Since Julia has never visited our home, she spends a few moments looking around, taking note of the children's artwork present on nearly every wall and the science experiments littering a corner of the kitchen counter. She smiles in my direction and I propose some tea while the men catch up on news in the living room and the children move outside to explore our play fort.

Julia looks unruffled and is wearing a form-fitting beige suit and less than sensible shoes. I wonder what impression I must make with negligible make up, multi-coloured T-shirt, battle-worn jeans and Birkenstocks. This thought is dispelled by the sparkle in Julia's eyes and her knowing smile. She is the same girl she was in university, a little finer-tuned perhaps but with the same warm acceptance of friends. We settle ourselves at the kitchen table, a little awkwardly at first, and take a moment to absorb each other's presence. We laugh at the absurdity of it.

"How are the kids?" I ask, breaking the moment's spell. I glance out the window at the children, smiling at the way they know how to settle in and feel comfortable with entirely new people.

"Great!" she answers quickly. "They're doing well in school and are growing so fast I hardly recognize them."

Trying to sound convincing, I reply, "I know what you mean."

She collects herself and adjusts her position on the chair. "How about yours?"

"Oh, they're good. Always on the run!"

"I don't know how you do it!" she exclaims. "I could never home-school my kids."

And here it is. I was wondering when this phrase would enter the conversation. Over the years I have heard it many times. "Well, it's something that feels really natural," and I launch into my familiar discourse. "It's more of a lifestyle."

Julia looks perplexed.

"It's just a way of life," I state. "The whole family embraces the idea that learning and living go hand in hand." I pause to catch my breath. "All of us pursue our own interests and we all feel that we're constantly gaining new ground. We take every chance we can to engage in activities that appeal to us each and every day." I smile. I hope I have been able to convey the spirit of our homeschooling experience.

"It sounds pretty good," she concedes. "But what about socialization? I would be concerned that the kids would be too isolated."

And there is the other chestnut. I laugh. "That's one of the main reasons we chose to homeschool! There seems to be so much negative socialization in our schools today that I just didn't feel comfortable sending them. You know—bullying and such. And since the kids are not in school, I think that perhaps they're better equipped for day-to-day social interactions. They can talk to anyone, regardless of age. They're used to it."

I glance at Julia to see if I can spy any reaction and decide to continue. "Since so many of our school's woes are coming to light, many more families are choosing to homeschool their kids. In our area, we have a terrific network of families to rely on for support and the kids have lots of friends who they see all the time." Because I have explained this matter to so many individuals over the years, I hope that my answer does not sound stale or defensive.

"So, there are many families in this area who homeschool?" Julia asks, sounding surprised.

"Oh yes! This little town of about 10,000 people has more than 75 families who homeschool."

Julia pauses to consider what I have presented. "But, how do you do it? Do you get books and syllabuses from the government or what?"

"You can do that, but we decided not to." I continue with, "In B.C., we have many choices. I tailor our homeschool year to the kid's personalities, combining their interests and abilities into a personalized plan rather than a 'one-size-fits-all' curriculum."

"Do you have to register with the government to let them know that you homeschool?" Julia inquires.

"Yes, in B.C. you must let the government know that you intend to homeschool your kids. What educational program you use is up to you. And I have to say, it is very reassuring to know that the government respects parents enough to allow them to make these choices for their own kids."

Julia ponders this prospect for a moment. "But what about being qualified to teach kids? Don't you need a teaching degree or something?" She appears to be feeling a little uncomfortable.

"No," I state calmly. "It's been my experience that a parent knows their own kids better than anyone else. And no one cares for their well being more. As times goes by, you discover exactly how your kids learn best. But, you have to do your homework. No one takes this job lightly."

Julia snorts at this statement. "Well, I can certainly tell you don't take this lightly! But, how do you find the time and keep up the energy?" She is smiling.

I grin back. "It feels so natural." I say, "Most days, especially at these ages, it feels like we're simply spending quality time together. Our days have a natural rhythm to them. Learning takes place everywhere and at any time of day."

"I listen to my own inner voice as well, don't get me wrong. I pursue my own interests regularly and our lifestyle is such that we all get lots of time to tackle what we want to tackle. Our routine gives the kids peace throughout the day, and my husband and I get to spend lots of time together in the evenings.

"Are the kids reading yet?" I sense that Julia already knows the answer. I consider how I should present this subject and decide to throw myself into it.

"Oh, yes." I sigh and momentarily look toward the children playing vigorously outside on the swing set. "And you may not believe this but, they taught themselves to read." I let this sink in for a bit before I continue. "I was careful to choose quality books that had the ability to transport the reader with words and I read to them a lot. I waited until they were ready for the alphabet and by using their love of movement, I incorporated the alphabet into our play-time. After they showed more interest, we played reading games. Before I knew it, they were reading by themselves." I stop and look hopefully in Julia's direction.

Julia absorbs what I have said and replies, "It never really occurred to me that learning to read could be such a natural experience. How about homeschooling kids of different ages and record keeping? How do you keep it all straight?"

"I do keep records but it isn't necessary since the academy I have registered with doesn't require it." I continue, "I have tons of scrapbooks loaded with the kids' projects through the years but I don't have to present it to any governmental agency or anything. As for homeschooling kids of different ages, I've always looked at the kids as individuals first. I know what each is capable of. I present material to each of them and gauge their understanding based on what their individual capabilities are."

On this final point, I sense that we are both tiring of this somewhat intense conversation and I move to change the subject. "But enough about me. How about you? How is work going?"

Julia informs me that she is now employed with an agricultural research organization in Calgary and enjoys the challenges of this work. She works full-time and employs a live-in nanny to maintain the house and provide after-school care for the children. Her life is secure and routine and she appears content with the way things are progressing.

Wishing to avoid additional illustrations of the differences between our two households, I watch for a break in the conversation to inquire about other old friends. Before long we are in the throes of reminiscing and are giggling just like the children.

On this happy note, we embrace and realize how much we are enjoying our reunion. We recognize that our life philosophies are poles apart but our friendship and respect for each other transcend any judgments. We feel genuinely secure with each other and know that we will always treat each other with fairness, understanding, acceptance and love.

Gently separating myself from her warm embrace, I propose a visit to the ocean.

"I'd love to!" Julia exclaims. "I've never been."

CONCLUSION

As long as the educational difficulties ingrained in many of today's institutions of traditional learning continue, parents must remain diligently focused on their crucial responsibilities to their own children. As we all know, children are the citizens of the future and as parents we have a duty to provide them with the basics necessary for a fulfilling tomorrow.

I feel that these basics (the original three R's) include the following:

- **Roots**. A child must be given a firm planting in the home, a keen sense of security and complete acceptance of self.
- **Reach**. A child must be encouraged to dream, to develop a vision, and to follow their aspirations.
- **Reason**. A child must be given unwavering support in their pursuit of the necessary tools that will guarantee they achieve their full potential.

I believe that the laying of this solid groundwork, coupled with an enriched and boundless childhood, will encourage our children to follow their deepest independent instincts and achieve ultimate happiness in their pursuit of *a* good life. By showering their path with inspiration and discovery and remaining flexible and open to possibility, I celebrate their journey to their ocean.

BIBLIOGRAPHY

Baldwin Dancy, Rahima. *You Are Your Child's First Teacher: What Parents Can Do With and For Their Children from Birth to Age Six.* Berkley, California: Celestial Arts, 1989

Corkille Briggs, Dorothy. *Your Child's Self-Esteem: Step-by-Step Guidelines for Raising Responsible, Productive, Happy Children.* New York: Doubleday, 1970

Gatto, John Taylor. *Dumbing Us Down: The Hidden Curriculum of Compulsory Schooling.* Gabriola Island, BC: New Society Publishers, 1992

Gatto, John Taylor. *The Underground History of American Education: A School Teacher's Intimate Investigation into the Problem of Modern Schooling.* Oxford, NY: Oxford Village Press, 2000

Griffith, Mary. *Homeschooling Handbook: From Preschool to High School, A Parent's Guide.* Rocklin, CA: Prima Publishing, 1999

Griffith, Mary. *The Unschooling Handbook: How to Use the Whole World as Your Child's Classroom.* Rocklin, CA: Prima Publishing, 1998

Holt, John and Pat Farenga. *Teach Your Own: The John Holt Book of Homeschooling.* Cambridge, MA: Perseus Publishing, 2003

Holt, John. *How Children Fail.* New York: Delacorte Press/Seymour Lawrence, 1995

Holt, John. *How Children Learn.* New York: Pitman Publishing Company, 1964

Holt, John. *Learning All The Time.* Reading, MA: Addison-Wesley Publishing Company, Inc., 1989

Kiyosaki, Robert T. *If You Want To Be Rich and Happy Don't Go To School: Ensuring Lifetime Security for Yourself and Your Children.* Fairfield, CT: Aslan Publishing, 1992

Neufeld, Gordon and Gabor Mate, M. D. *Hold on to Your Kids: Why Parents need to Matter More Than Peers.* Ballantine Books, 2005

Olsen, Darcy Ann. *Universal Preschool Is Not Golden Ticket: Why Government Should Not Enter The Preschool Business.* Washington, DC: Cato Institute, 1999

Suarez, Paul and Gena. *Homeschooling Methods: Seasoned Advice on Learning Styles.* Nashville, Tennessee: B. and H. Publishing Group, 2006

Willis, Mariaemma, M.S. and Victoria Kindle Hodson, M.A. *Discover Your Child's Learning Style: Children Learn in Unique Ways—Here's the Key to Every Child's Learning Success.* Roseville, CA: Prima Publishing, 1999

WEBSITES

adrianbruce.com

aplusmath.com

auntieray.co.uk

babybirdproductions.com

charlottemasonhomeschooling.wordpress.com

christopherushomeschool.org

discoveryeducation.com

edhelper.com

freemathhelp.com

holtgws.com

kaboose.com

kidport.com

kindbook.com

primarygames.com

proteacher.net

superkids.com

themathworksheetsite.com

Printed in Great Britain
by Amazon